THE WILDER

ESSAYS ON CONTEMPORARY MORMON THOUGHT

THE WILDERNESS OF FAITH

ESSAYS ON CONTEMPORARY MORMON THOUGHT

Edited by
John Sillito

Signature Books   Salt Lake City   1991

For B. F. Cummings III

COVER ILLUSTRATION: *MARCH 21,* BY MARILYN MILLER, 1988, SERIGRAPH
COVER DESIGN: JULIE EASTON

∞ Printed on acid free paper

95   94   93   92   91   6   5   4   3   2   1

Library of Congress Cataloging-in-Publication Data

The Wilderness of faith: essays on contemporary Mormon thought / edited by John Sillito.
    p.   cm.
    ISBN 1-56085-009-4
    1. Mormon Church—Doctrines. 2. Church of Jesus Christ of Latter-Day Saints—Doctrines.
  I. Sillito, John R.
BX8637.W65 1990
289.3'32—dc20
          90-20514
          CIP

CONTENTS

EDITOR'S INTRODUCTION

> The autonomy of conscience must be asserted. It is not a
> fragment of divinity, an outpost of God or anything foreign
> to the nature of the individual himself. It is the implement
> of free agency, and exists in its own right.... A well struc-
> tured conscience acts independently even when it assents
> and agrees.
>
> In the growth of the mind, the most precious growth is
> that of conscience, the decision-making structure of our be-
> ing. Eternal progress is ... the continuous process of ex-
> panding capacity to make moral judgments.
> —B. F. Cummings III (*The Eternal Individual Self*
>   [Salt Lake City, 1968], 123-24)

I FIRST ENCOUNTERED THE TEACHINGS OF BENJAMIN F. CUMMINGS
as a young convert to Mormonism, when he was my Sunday school
teacher in Salt Lake City's Liberty Ward. I didn't realize then that
this elderly and gentle man was a noted linguist, teacher, and philosopher—that knowledge came later. And while his views on Mormon
theology were far more advanced than my own, I learned two important lessons from him: the necessity of always seeking for additional
insight and the legitimacy of questioning from within the fold.

This collection of essays is concerned with the demands of
faith in a period of great change. The majority were written during
the decade of the 1980s, a time when Mormons seemed particularly

challenged to make sense of their faith in the light of developments within and without the church. The contributors represent some of the most thoughtful and perceptive of a particulary talented generation of Mormon thinkers. Drawing upon their traditions and amplifying them in terms of contemporary realities, the contributors to this book address many of the most central concerns of our time. Some of the essays are very personal, exploring questions ranging from the loss of a child to the exercise of personal spiritual gifts. Others examine developments within Mormon culture from the impact of bureaucracy to Mormonism's relationship to the larger society.

All the essays are written from within the Mormon world view which, as Ed Firmage notes, recognizes that "a religious community must also respect individuals even as it preserves core beliefs of the community." Central to these essays is the concept articulated by Lavina Fielding Anderson of "mature obedience." As Anderson observes, such obedience is "motivated by love not fear. It has to be deeply rooted in a testimony of the redemptive sacrifice of the Savior . . . It is not an exchange of responsibilities and duties but the interplay, complexity, and richness of an ongoing intimate powerful relationship."

Also central is the notion that contemporary Mormonism needs a loyal opposition within its ranks. As Elouise Bell observes: "The concept of valued opposition is not, I fear, very well understood in Mormon culture. And without it we cause ourselves and others needless grief and may actually hinder what we would advance."

Unfortunately, Bell is right and one goal of this book is to make better known the value of such a loyal opposition in the church. Too often we see such individuals as unthinking critics or dissenters who seek only to tear down. Dissent is not a bad word nor a negative concept. Indeed I think the opposite is true. I have long admired Norman Thomas, the Presbyterian minister who became the leader of the Socialist party and its six-time candidate for president. In his book *Great Dissenters* (New York: W. W. Norton, 1961), he wrote: "The secret of a good life is to have the right loyalties and to hold them in the right scale of values. The value of dissent and dissenters is to make us reappraise those values with supreme concern for the truth" (13).

Of course dissent per se is not necessarily a virtue. But neither is conformity, complacency, or apathy. We live in a society of conservatism and affluence that fosters a generally suspicious view of dissenters within our ranks be that the church or the body politic. At the same time those of us who are committed to questioning and dialogue must have tolerance for the views of others. Too often I forget something Frank C. Robertson, the Mormon western writer, wrote in his autobiography *A Ram in the Thicket* (New York: Hastings House, 1959). Quoting his "preacher grandfather" who cautioned that "orthodoxy is my doxy; heterodoxy is your doxy," Robertson observed that before we criticize others for their opinions we should remember that "where there is no heresy, there is no liberty" (272).

In the 1960s we used to say, "If you aren't part of the solution then you're part of the problem." The essays in this book are meant to advance solutions, not make problems. I like to think they represent the views of the very best of today's loyal opposition— though not everyone whose work is included here might accept that label. On balance, these essayists—writing from various realms of commitment—embody the autonomy of conscience and the capacity to make moral judgements that B. F. Cummings so eloquently advocated.

I appreciate the following publications for permission to reproduce, sometimes in different form, the selections contained herein: to *Sunstone* for the essays of Arthur R. Bassett, Irene M. Bates, Elouise M. Bell, D. Jeff Burton, Richard J. Cummings, Edwin B. Firmage, Scott G. Kenney, L. Jackson Newell, Levi S. Peterson, and Donlu D. Thayer; and to *Dialogue: a Journal of Mormon Thought* for the essays of Lavina Fielding Anderson, Betina Lindsey, and Susan B. Taber. Two essays—"Two Churches of Mormonism," by Ron Molen, and "The Ghost of the Pioneer Woman," by Linda Sillitoe—are published here for the first time. In addition, I appreciate the support of the staff of Signature Books whose diligent work has guaranteed that the essays contained in this book will be made available to a wider audience.

1.
Restoring the Church: Zion in the Nineteenth and Twenty-first Centuries

Edwin B. Firmage

THE MORMON PEOPLE AND PROPHETS SENSED FROM THE BEGINning that our religion would work only in community. Peculiar Mormon teachings did not simply demand their own institutions; radical social innovations such as polygamy and the United Order required a unique lifestyle and community. We can say now in retrospect that a separate Mormon system of law and society was necessary to protect our vision against hostile government and inadequate law. Beyond that, however, Joseph Smith and Brigham Young understood that for religion to be effective it must be woven into every warp and weft of our lives. No laws of God are temporal only; all are spiritual. If this is to be, the community must allow the introjection of spirituality into the law to enliven the community with God's spirit.

For Joseph Smith and Brigham Young this vision, in its highest level of effectiveness at least, demanded a gathered church: Zion. This vision was absolutely central for both of them, so much so that they led us into an unequal, nearly hopeless struggle. And yet long after Zion should have been obliterated by an industrial state and national markets, its institutions flourished. Mormon law and courts existed with vitality into the twentieth century. Survival demanded accommodation with the national community, even if it meant abandoning the distinctive and controversial practices of communal economics, polygamy, and theocratic government.

With the powerful literalism of commoners, the Mormons, its lay leaders indistinguishable in education and social position from other church members, set out to make Zion a reality. Brigham exhorted with characteristic pungency, "I have Zion in my view constantly. We are not going to wait for angels or for Enoch and his company to come and build Zion, but we are going to build it" (in *Journal of Discourses*, 26 vols. [London: Latter-day Saints Book Depot, 1854-86], 9:28). His counselor and friend, Jedediah M. Grant, exclaimed, "If you want a heaven, go to and make it" (ibid., 3:66).

Self-serving individualism, particularly when motivated by wealth, was severely sanctioned. Like ancient Israel's, the Mormon communal vision was all-encompassing. Looking forward to a return to Jackson County, Missouri, the center stake of Zion, Brigham warned in 1865, "If this people neglect their duty, turn away from the holy commandments which God has given us, seek for their own individual wealth, and neglect the interests of the Kingdom of God, we may expect to be here quite a while — perhaps a period that will be for longer than we anticipated" (ibid., 11:102).

The hallmark of Mormonism was and is this vital and powerful communal cohesion. The power undergirding Mormon communality is reinforced by factors in addition to the theological vision of Zion. The trek to the Great Basin and the colonial experience of settling a major part of western America welded Mormons together with unbreakable bonds. There they built Zion in mountain-encircled valleys. They had consummated one of the great migrations of American history in a self-conscious pattern of the camp of Israel. Brigham extended Zion's tent with stakes implanted from San Bernardino to Old Mexico, throughout much of California, Nevada, Idaho, Arizona, and New Mexico — a rugged, at times brutal experience made possible by a shared vision of Zion. The authoritarian structure inherent in such an endeavor was helpful, perhaps indispensable, and probably inevitable.

The uncoerced social affinity essential to the legitimacy of Mormon community was powerfully strengthened, not shattered, by persecution. The federal government began a half-hearted campaign against the Mormons with ineffective legislation against polygamy and then attempted to eradicate the practice by enforcing laws with heartless brutality. Simultaneously the government attacked Mormon civil rights and liberties, including the rights to serve on juries, to emigrate, to vote, and to hold office. Finally the government waged war on Mormon society and corporate personhood by seeking to disenfranchise the church.

The effect of all this was to cement the Mormon community into an impregnable whole. Mormons survived initial persecution and developed the bones and sinews of a people, as did Israel in exodus. They grew under intense and protracted persecution and matured in isolation. But great costs were paid. The combined effect of overt federal persecution and the more thorough and irresistible subversion of Mormon society by widespread industrialization and encroaching national markets finally obliterated much that was unique. Nevertheless, a distinctive Mormon culture survived — part religious community, part ethnic group. Mormonism has powerful characteristics of both church and tribe.

The nineteenth-century Mormon experience can only be described as heroic. Our challenge as we approach the twenty-first century is to continue with equal integrity. This cannot be done by attempting to repeat the past nor by continuing traditions appropriate to continental migrations, colonization, and resistance to persecution. The courage of our founders can be approached only with the same robust vitality that empowered Mormons of the nineteenth century to break decisively with the culture of their time.

Like our individual strengths and dominant characteristics, our corporate strength of intense communality possesses a shadow that we deny at our peril. We have inherited the shadow of our parents' nineteenth-century traditions of great strength, not simply the traditions themselves. If we recognize this we have nothing to fear; if we do not, we will descend into a parody of the past, devoid of its integrity. We must examine the characteristics of our intense communal insularity and authoritarianism, particularly as they reinforce chauvinistic, ethnocentric tendencies that are no longer valuable in our dissent from the larger national culture.

The challenge for the LDS church in the twenty-first century must be to forge common bonds not to accentuate differences. Our characteristics of both church and ethnic group must be acknowledged. The characteristics of church possess the regenerative power to change our lives toward God's image — saving grace. Those of ethnic tribalism do not.

Military-like discipline may have been needed to colonize a hostile frontier, but it is an obstruction to conversion, not a helpful invitation to mature spirituality. Conversion occurs from the center outward; external coercion does not help the process. We need to move from authoritarian ethnocentricity to a church of Jesus and Paul. When worship of community displaces worship of God, we accentuate our idiosyncrasy by self-love and self-worship. When we worship God we proceed inward to our center and outward in identification with all the human family and all life. We love as God loves. Nevertheless, the empowerment possible only with the church *in community* must be preserved. The religious teachings and practices of the church can only become real in community. Outside community such teachings remain strangely disembodied—ideas that have little effect on our lives. Church without community is impotent. Community without church places itself rather than God at the center, resulting in an unregenerating tribal culture.

The church in the first century after Christ also faced this crisis, and the Pauline solution points the way for every Christian community that followed. The Christian idea took flesh in community—an intense, insular, Jewish community. For some time it seemed inconceivable that Christianity could exist outside the Jewish matrix in which it was born; but Paul had a vision. Paul came to see that the sociology of Judaism was not prerequisite to the Christian idea. Christianity could be embodied in other cultures, all culture, and Jesus, not the Jewish law, was the gateway. This vision precipitated so great a crisis in the church that the first conference in Christian history was called at Jerusalem. After much discussion the Pauline vision was accepted. The enormous struggle to realize that vision ultimately cost Paul his life, but henceforth the direction of the church was outward—to the entire Roman world and beyond.

No greater burden than the *necessary* core of the Christian message should be required of the community as a condition for accepting and living the Christian idea. Any Christian community exporting the gospel cannot require the investigating group to accept the sociology of the community presenting the message. The grafting culture must be given the same freedom enjoyed by the exporting group: to nourish the Christian message within their own cultural tradition.

Of course some social practices in any culture may be anti-thetical to the Christian message. Other customs may be more or less conducive to Christian flowering, but each culture must receive freedom sufficient to make these experiments and reach its own conclusions. The alternative is cultural imperialism in the guise of Christian evangelization.

The dialogue within Christianity as to what constitutes the necessary core message continues in every generation and in every community where the message is introduced. The process compels openness and outwardness even in fiercely insular communities resisting every step—unless, of course, they give way to idolatrous, ethnocentric self-worship. God is then displaced with the communal self which grows in its own image, accentuating every group charac-teristic in perfect caricature.

This dialogue on core essentials exists not only between contemporaneous communities but also between generations within the same community. The gradual change within a believing com-munity obscures the evidence of the evolutionary process, but the process can be seen starkly by separating the centuries.

Accordingly I would like to examine here the Mormon ex-perience in the nineteenth century and contrast it with our situa-tion now as we approach the twenty-first century. What follows are examples of persistent nineteenth-century practices which I believe Mormonism will have to confront as it embraces a differ-ent time and other cultures. By no means is this a challenge to the spiritual core of either Christianity or Mormonism. Rather it is an invitation to discover and distinguish our core spiritual principles from the sociological matrix in which we happen to live at a particular time and place. The former we hold and revere; the latter we change as circumstance reveals to us the wisdom of doing so.

The inherited gift of intense community has a tendency to enthrone any peculiar communal characteristic as if it were a divine absolute. This is particularly true for Mormons because of a peculiar insight that paradoxically should produce openness but if un-examined results in the opposite—the open canon. Joseph Smith believed that God could and would give revelatory messages to the world, revealing himself in every age and among many peoples. With a liberality of spirit that even now seems starkly modern, he taught that the Jewish and early Christian scripture was holy but not perfect or inerrant and surely not complete. God had spoken and would yet speak to many groups. The result of this insight should have been and to some extent has been that we avoid the presumptuousness of creeds which tightly define and confine God and our relationship to him. Every generation and people wants to be left with great freedom to explore that awesome mystery. Such people, one would think, would never presume formally or informally to excommunicate each other — to pronounce anathema — because someone saw another way.

Over time, however, Mormons developed an idea of a de facto infallibility concerning prophetic pronouncements. The authoritarian tendencies developed in our early community building were inappropriately transferred to doctrinal areas and ecclesiastical government. Although Joseph Smith denied any notion of infallibility or inerrancy, even for the biblical canon, we have come perilously close to believing in the infallibility of the comments of LDS religious leaders, however casual and unexamined.

Like any other religious community, we can all too easily see God's benediction upon, perhaps even his hand in creating, our every social more. Our group customs — for example, our predilection for conservative politics and classical, marketplace economics — become hallowed, divine. If this process continues unchallenged and unexamined, we begin to worship ourselves, not God. We enthrone every social peculiarity as being revelatory. We defend and accentuate every custom and cling to them through time. Customs of a particular time and place, perhaps defensible or at least understandable near the time of origin, become increasingly grotesque as we carry them into another age.

A painful example illustrates this phenomenon. Early Mormons originally came in large numbers from New England and the East. These displaced Puritans carried with them healthy notions of abolitionist sentiment. In Missouri some blacks were evangelized, baptized, and ordained to priesthood office like other converts. Understandably, slave-owning Missourians were frightened. As a self-defensive measure of preservation in an increasingly violent environment, the Mormons agreed to desist from evangelizing among slaves. Over time, probably unevenly at first, the ordination of blacks to priesthood office ceased.

In time the origin of the policy was forgotten. Given the Mormon belief in continuing public revelation, we increasingly bestowed upon this expedient practice a revelatory status. Later Brigham Young and subsequent church leaders made perfectly indefensible statements to justify the practice long after its evolutionary origins were lost. A wretched theology of sorts grew up around a practice that was antithetical to Christian teaching. Paradoxically an early Mormon insight was lost—that abolitionism and Christian equality were consistent with God's universal parenthood and our universal brotherhood and sisterhood—and a belief in continuing revelation was turned on its head.

Although that practice has now thankfully been reversed, its history is a good study in the potential dysfunctions of the community. Our notion of revealed truth must be moderated, indeed bounded, by the realization that we perceive God's will through the filter of our own subjectivity, our imperfection, our humanity. Without this insight, that which should liberate imprisons: outworn practice becomes new dogma, more rigid, not adaptable to changing circumstance. When the concept of revelation is joined by a notion of prophetic infallibility, a dogmatic system is born that eventually becomes excessively authoritarian, ironically imprisoning a people in the past when the revelatory notion was meant to free them from the past.

Similarly we have adopted a means of succession to the presidency of the LDS church based on length of apostolic tenure which insures that this vital office once held by the youthful Joseph will almost always be held by someone of extreme old age. Yet no authoritative doctrinal precept mandates this. Over time custom hardened into rule, and now church government is enfeebled at senior levels in the Council of the Twelve and the First Presidency. Nothing in church doctrine forbids an emeritus status for members of the Quorum of the Twelve. This would insure younger leadership in the Council of the Twelve and in the person of the president of the church. Apostolic succession to the presidency still based on tenure could continue but with individuals at least a decade younger assuming the presidency. Or better yet, members of the Council of the Twelve might select the president from among themselves.

At this point another early Mormon characteristic with its accompanying twentieth-century shadow appears: We accept a greater degree of authoritarian leadership than would most people living in a modern industrial and democratic state. Undoubtedly this authority is legitimate. It is uncoerced, flowing naturally from a group as homogeneous and communal as ours.

But a religious community must also respect individuals even as it preserves the core beliefs of the community. We believe in uncreated intelligence: a soul sovereign and co-eternal with God: "I was in the beginning with the Father, and am the Firstborn. . . . Ye were also in the beginning with the Father. . . . Man was also in the beginning with God. Intelligence, or the light of truth, was not created or made, neither indeed can be. . . . Behold, here is the agency of man" (D&C 93:21, 23, 29, 31). This should allow—demand—an enormous respect for each other's belief, our individual vision, even in community. Prophetic leadership should consciously decry any notion of infallibility of leader or scripture.

If we believe this then egalitarian dialogue should be encouraged with full heart. This would include searching, open, and honest examination of our history and our scripture. "Honest" and "faithful" history would be the same. Mormon teachings and practices would be discussed and opinions sought at all levels. The profoundly energizing Mormon practice of lay priesthood would be lived more fully than it is currently, with even less distinction between clergy and laity. Theological notions or church practice would be discussed with great openness in every class and quorum. Any creed-like attempt to confine God to something as tiny as our minds would be greeted with good humor. Authoritarian pronouncement would be made infrequently and with caution. All women would be invited into full priesthood participation with every quorum and office in the church open to them. No doctrine of which I am aware forbids this. The absence of feminine spirituality in the councils of church government is a loss of such enormity in Christian history as to be impossible to overstate. With other Christian traditions Mormons must no longer ignore this open wound.

By not decreasing authoritarian tendencies within Mormonism, we risk spiritual and moral infantilism or at best adolescence—a dependence on others for inner spiritual and moral structure which prevents our own robust maturity. Notions of lay priesthood assume that for most purposes we need no intermediary between ourselves and God save Christ. One may be our spokesperson, to be sure, at the pulpit or before the altar. But he or she acts for us all. On another occasion we might be the voice. No difference in kind exists. This is the mature form of Christian belief that can take us into the next century, growing in likeness of God, not ourselves.

How do we get there? Perhaps the Pauline example contains the key. A burgeoning church spilling beyond our mountain enclave will face challenges in crossing each frontier. With each barrier we cross, we will become more a church and less an ethnic group. If simultaneously we maintain our core beliefs, our communalism will remain intact but more refined.

This growth will bring with it paradox. As we attempt to save our brothers and sisters in the Third World, perhaps they will save us. As Mormon missionaries evangelize people in South and Central America, Asia, and Africa, we constantly will be forced to decide what portion of our message is social custom from Kanosh, Kanab, and Kanarraville, or the essence of Christianity.

Our lay priesthood is an enormous advantage. We cannot impose foreign clergy on native communities for long. At the very least, we should train native lay leaders and ordain them within months. We cannot impose full religious and cultural imperialism on a community in which the entire congregation at every level of leadership is governed from among themselves. If we listen, they will teach us.

The issues will be many: African or Tongan drums in religious ceremonies, forms of dress and food, appropriateness of practices or teachings in a radically new environment, marriage customs. Poverty in the Third and Fourth Worlds will be our great teacher. Our cultural notions of the government's role in a nation's economy will be called into question and appropriately discarded by many nations. Our wealth blinds us; their poverty may remove the scales from our eyes. A core Christian gospel will emerge, "these necessary things," uncluttered with our own sociological baggage.

Similarly as Mormonism enters Communist countries in Eastern Europe and eventually China, we will find that our own enthnocentric notions, however dear to us, are not essential to the gospel's core.

Within our own country the growth of Mormonism in large urban areas among diverse racial and ethnic groups will force a dialogue upon us and within us. The result, I hope, will be a different sort of community: richer in texture, more diverse, less authoritarian.

Perhaps we can enter into interfaith dialogue with our Christian and non-Christian brothers and sisters, not seeing them primarily as potential converts but as disciples like ourselves. We might give more attention to converting ourselves to the truths they possess. Mormonism's influence for good in the world will be much greater, I suspect, among the many who remain firmly attached to their own religious tradition rather than within the relative few who join our faith.

We trivialize God when we see all history pointing toward New York in the 1820s. Our own community becomes too short, too narrow, too thin. Sociologist Robert Bellah's "community of memory" must extend for us before the nineteenth century (see Bellah, R. Madsen, William Sullivan, A. Swidler, and S. M. Tipton, *Habits of the Heart* [New York: Harper & Row, 1985]). In the next century as our Mormon community moves outward into Africa, South and Central America, and Asia, we will likely expand in time as well. Mormons who think that God ceased to speak some time after the first century of the Christian era and resumed dialogue with us in the nineteenth century ignore centuries rich in the continuing story of God's relationship with us all. That bleak picture of utter apostasy is hardly brightened by seeing a few preparatory acts as God's prologue to the Restoration.

Alternatively we can choose to see God's message in the writings of Christian fathers and mothers through the centuries as wonderful messages complete in themselves. A vital sense of continuity is lost for Mormons, who generally are closed to such literature and history. The Latin and Greek fathers, the writings and meditations of Christian mystics from the first century to the present, reformers within and without the dominant church of a time and place: all reveal the mystery of God's relationship with us.

Beyond Christianity the Jewish tradition, Buddhism, Hinduism, Taoism, and the Islamic tradition have a richness to offer us. We may gain invaluable richness from an inward journey, not into cultural ethnocentricity but to the center of our own soul. We Mormons have excelled in the outward journey as colonizers and organizers, making deserts blossom, but too many of our hearts may remain an arid desert. Christian and non-Christian mystical traditions have much to share with us, more in corrective ways than as replacements for our traditions. Taken alone the mystical tradition could result in an other-worldliness divorced from human need and social action. Equally true social activism shorn of direction from our spiritual center could produce even greater injustice. A dynamic balance between spiritual meditation and action for social justice is the ideal.

Our view and use of scripture could expand as well. Overwhelmingly we now see the Bible as a proof text, using isolated passages to prove a particular teaching, and pass this off as pastoral instruction in scripture. What loss. This is strange too because formally we do not accept the fundamentalist belief in scriptural inerrancy, nor do we see the scriptures as a source of priesthood empowerment as in the Protestant tradition. As we sense our own need for real nourishment, we may move toward non-dogmatic, non-apologetic study of the Bible simply to gain the richness of its real message.

We would aid this process greatly by diminishing our monopolistic use of the King James version of the Bible. This beautiful English translation is a treasure beyond price. But thousands of documents are now available and have been for decades which the King James translators did not have. And our language has changed dramatically. If we want the scriptures to come alive for us and for our children, we should embrace new translations. Again it is strange that a people who rejected Protestant fundamentalism toward scripture in the nineteenth century should seek so avidly to board a ship in this century that is so clearly sinking as is this form of scriptural fundamentalism, relegating scriptures to the status of an icon: something to be venerated but not understood. Our choice of a Bible translation too must turn outward. If not we remain cut off from much dialogue in biblical research and from greater meaning and sensitivity in biblical education. Of course Joseph Smith used the King James translation; what other translation would he use? After one wades through all the rationalizations for our current practice, this is the fundamental reason for retaining this translation, and it is not sufficient.

I suspect that even something as central and sacred in Mormon teaching as the role of the family will come under scrutiny as we move into the next century. It seems reasonable to believe that loving

family associations formed in mortality may continue in the resurrection. But retaining the absolute centrality of the family in our
beliefs can cause us to miss a much bigger picture. Millions of single
and divorced people can be hurt, feeling that they are only margin-
ally involved in church participation. It is possible to make an icon
of the family as easily as a particular version of the Bible.

Jesus in his own life and teachings revealed a much grander
vision. In almost every example of family association in his life and
ministry, Jesus taught us to transcend the family. The family relationship was often used by him as a negative example — that is, he taught
that if our sense of love and obligation did not move beyond family
and blood relationships, we had not yet perceived his message.
When his family found him in the temple, he responded to Mary's
mild rebuke by saying that he was about his Father's business — not
theirs (Luke 2:41-50). When informed that his mother and brothers
were outside, he told a crowded room that his disciples were his
family (Matt. 12:46-50). In an intentionally harsh statement so we
would not miss the point, he responded to a disciple's request to
bury his father, "Let the dead bury the dead" (8:21-22). There is no
reliable historical evidence that Jesus ever married. His disciples
forsook all and followed him (I hope they did not desert their families, but the record does not clearly demonstrate that they did not).

The journey outward is not so much toward individualism,
though that is part of it. The individual must be free from coercive,
demeaning authoritarianism if he or she is to mature spiritually into
responsible autonomy. If the community is too insular, this process
of individuation can take place only by breaking outside. The journey outward, however, is primarily a journey into larger community,
larger in time and space. We will come to identify ourselves with
Christians beyond the Mormon experience, those living now and
those who have gone before. With believers in traditions other than
Christianity, we see similarities in the human quest that are more
fundamental than our differences. Part of this recognition may
come as we travel inward on the meditative journey to our own
center or outward as we graft into our community of memory others
from radically different cultures.

Jesus' life and message transcended community, race, gender, nationality, tribe, even family. If we trivialize this message, we
violate the first commandment by some form of self-worship. Ethno-

centricity indeed has power. Religion in community is the spiritual word embodied. But ethnocentricity alone is communal self-worship. The refining process of God's grace is in the true religious experience with God at the center.

Jesus broke traditional bonds. He recognized that his message would set children against parents, brothers and sisters against their kin. But the same message has the power to bind them up again, united across differences of race, gender, nationality, religious traditions even through time. His parable of the Good Samaritan; his teaching of having no place to lay his head or to lodge; his refusal to eat or converse only with "good people"; the first great crisis of Christianity, that of resolving Jewish and Gentile Christianity through the Pauline paradigm — all point the way.

Jesus preached and practiced a transcendent message of self-love, love of neighbor, and finally love of enemy. Neighbor and enemy combined such that no one was excluded from our love. On our inner journey of Christian meditation, on our outer journey to transcend race, gender, and nationality, Mormonism must and will overleap the mountain redoubt that nurtured us in our infancy. With the Puritans across the continent in an earlier age, with Joseph and Brigham, Augustine and Paul, we continue our search for the City of God.

2.
The Ambiguous Gift of Obedience

Lavina Fielding Anderson

IT STRIKES ME THAT MORMON INTELLECTUALS CONSTITUTE A genuine subculture within the larger host culture of Mormonism. We have our own heroes, mentors, and martyrs. We have our own publications. The Sunstone Symposia, meetings of the Society for the Sociological Study of Mormon Life, the Association for Mormon Letters, and the Mormon History Association are, if not general conferences, at least specific conferences. Many of us have come to assume a minimum number of common beliefs—for instance, that a search for the truth does not simultaneously preclude a search for the facts and that loving the church and living within it do not eliminate either freedom or the pain and joy which result from exercising that freedom.

That is why the issue of obedience is so unquestionably timely and why I want to reflect in a personal way on what obedience means to people like me. I am assuming for the purposes of this essay that most readers are people like me. At some point in the temple we made a covenant of obedience, which moves the whole question beyond the simple level enjoined in the scriptures upon any Christian. We renew this covenant from time to time, and it may come to our minds with particular force when certain events occur. I think, for instance, of the obedient silence of Gene England, teaching Mormon ethics at the Stanford Institute of Religion, when his superiors passed on instructions that he was no longer to discuss Vietnam. I also think of the instructions to ecclesiastical leaders in

Linda King Newell's and Valeen Tippitts Avery's areas not to invite them to speak on church history topics — instructions that reflected official displeasure with their triple-prizewinning biography of Emma Hale Smith. Other readers are no doubt familiar with similar examples.

Examples like these clearly pose the dilemma of obedience for people like me. As cases they have the virtue of being behavioral: we can tell if someone is being obedient by what he or she actually does. We do not come up with those particular behaviors on our own; we are being obedient to an external requirement. These imposed requirements have prompted the indignant question from some friends: "Why do you put up with that?" Such a question implies that the questioner would simply remove himself or herself from the situation in which such a requirement might be made.

There is a great deal of talk about "unrighteous dominion," integrity, and violations of free agency when such occasions arise. The situation is, of course, more complicated than that. I have found it helpful to recall in addition to scriptures on unrighteous dominion, other scriptures fraught with equal ambiguity: God's patience with what clearly seems to be Gideon's sign-seeking using bedewed and dry fleeces (Judges 6) or God's seeming impatience with the quite natural question of Zacharias in the temple about his future fatherhood. I remember the terrible test of Abraham's obedience, where Abraham and Isaac, together willing to fulfill God's commandment, found instead a ram in a thicket. I contrast their experience with that of Jephtah, judge of Israel, who vowed to sacrifice the first thing he met returning from what he hoped would be the deliverance of his people. That thing was his daughter — his only child. She, like Isaac, was willing that the vow be fulfilled, but there was no ram in the thicket for her (Judges 11). What do these examples tell us about obedience?

One observation forced upon us by the ambiguity of experience is that there are always at least two points of view in play. Mormon historian D. Michael Quinn talks about "God's truth," the truth upon which "man's truth" must break if there is a conflict ("Quinn Responds," *Dialogue: A Journal of Mormon Thought* 18 [Fall 1985]: 13). His splendid essay, "LDS Church Authority and New Plural Marriages, 1890-1904" (in *Dialogue: A Journal of Mormon Thought* 18 [Spring 1985]: 9-105), documents in detail the painful breaking of one truth against another. I think of Nephi and his rebellious brothers in the Book of Mormon. Nephi was always right, obnoxiously right; his brothers were — granted — snivellers, selfish, and small-minded but also had some justification for feeling "oppressed" by a brother who wished to dominate and rule over them, always getting his own way. Despite numerous debates of their two positions, which Nephi himself records, it is Father Lehi who is most enlightening for me. "Ye have accused him," he tells his two elder sons, "that he sought power and authority over you; but I know that he hath not sought for power nor authority over you, but he hath sought the glory of God, *and your own eternal welfare*" (2 Ne. 1:25; emphasis added). Could it be that the person we perceive as oppressing and dominating us is really actuated by concern for our eternal welfare?

A second observation is that whenever an organization exists, this same ambiguous question of obedience will also exist. Part of growing up is learning to accept this ambiguity. Peter and the other apostles boldly declared before the Sanhedrin: "We ought to obey God rather than men" (Acts 5:29). Agreed. There is wonderful clarity in seeing the angel yourself, hearing the voice yourself, receiving the vision yourself. But whenever the word of God is transmitted through another, we must decide as individuals whether he or she is telling the truth — God's truth, not just wishful thinking or self-deception. Whenever the word of God is transmitted through an organization, the question will inevitably arise: Am I obeying God or am I obeying human beings? Without going through the arduous process of seeking revelation for ourselves upon the point in question (which we all are enjoined to do) and receiving confirmation (which rests in God's good pleasure and which we may not control), we cannot be sure whether the ultimate source of a particular commandment is in fact God or rather human beings.

We can explore questions of obedience not only in the scriptures but also within our own history as an organization. In so doing, we must observe that the social context in which our obedience is asked for and given has changed dramatically. I'd like to label the difference in these two changes prompt obedience and informed obedience. Prompt obedience does not mean that questioning does not accompany a command or that it is not obeyed without pain. Such questionings and pains are, however, private. The process of prompt obedience does not acknowledge them nor allow for their incorporation into the process of obeying the directive. This type of obedience is sometimes called blind obedience, but I regret the negative connotations it has acquired and prefer an alternative appellation.

My illustrations of this principle may seem stereotypical, but that is because they have entered our folk culture as symbols rather than as specific events. We hear stories of how Brigham Young would have a list of names read from the pulpit in conference; and whatever their private situations and feelings, a score of men would leave their families for missions. Brother Brigham has a brief conversation with another family, and it would leave its home and farm for a new settlement. We look at such manifestations of obedience and wonder, Would I have done that? *Could* I have done that? Should *they* have done that? Was Brigham Young arbitrary? Were the Saints mindless sheep? The questions come close to the bone as we remember the Mountain Meadows massacre.

In asking such questions, we stand clearly in the late twentieth century, not the nineteenth. We forget the kind of personal relationship which existed between Brigham Young and his people. This kind of intense intimacy no longer exists among the General Authorities, let alone between the prophet and the mass of Saints today. It is hard to analogize the same fealty Brigham's people must have felt for him and the union they felt with him—feelings which I believe he reciprocated—when most of us can no longer even name all of the General Authorities let alone recognize them, remember conversations with them, or even recall memorable sermons from each. We relate to an image—in many cases a polished and conventional image—reflected by the official publications and the careful formality of general conferences. The Public Relations Department speaks for the church, and the realm in which General Authorities express opinions in public is a narrow one. The church is too big, its bureaucracy is too big, for the trust which comes from personal relationships.

We also need to accept that much of the functioning of the church is the functioning of a bureaucracy. Why then should we be surprised when it acts like a bureaucracy? Joseph Smith announced an essential principle when he explained that "a prophet was a prophet only when he was acting as such" (*History of the Church*, 2d. ed., ed. B. H. Roberts [Salt Lake City: Deseret Book,

1950], 5:265). Similarly General Authorities who are also managers of departments are apostles or seventies only when they are acting as such, and that does not necessarily include all of the times they are acting as managers. The same can be said of stake presidents and bishops. Sometimes they act as administrators and sometimes as stewards. I feel that being able to distinguish between the two functions is extremely useful.

Furthermore, our segment of the twentieth century is characterized by a distrust of organizations and institutions. We think of Helmut Huebner standing against the great betrayal of the Third Reich, of Richard M. Nixon's betrayal of the American presidency. There is less trust now in doctors, judges, police officers. In some ways this is good because people must take responsibility for thinking through issues and making informed decisions.

Applied to the church, this condition produces what I called "informed obedience." In the church context, however, it has mixed results. Let me tell two stories. A friend of mine in the Pacific Northwest told me recently that his elders' quorum president had advised quorum members to sign up for a service project. They would be gone from their homes from Friday afternoon until late Saturday and were to bring hammers, saws, screwdrivers, and other construction tools. My friend wanted to know more: What was the project? Where was it? Who was it for? Did it involve just their quorum or other quorums in the stake? Was this the quorum president's idea or was he acting on instructions from someone else? My friend explained, "I work about sixty hours a week. I have a wife and a new baby. If the church wants my whole weekend, I have a right to know why." He also mentioned that he had been involved in service projects before which had been unnecessary: repairing homes for people whose monthly incomes exceeded his own, helping move people who did not require it and had done no planning so many hours were wasted, and so on. The quorum president refused to respond to these questions or those of the others in the group. There was considerable confusion and resentment. My friend did not sign up.

This situation raises some questions. Should my friend have swallowed his questions and decided that the quorum president would be responsible for his resentments? Should he have prayed until he felt better about accepting the assignment? What is the responsibility of leaders in such cases?

The second story shows a useful contrast, I feel. It demonstrates the operating style of Cathy Stokes, president of the Hyde Park Ward Relief Society in Chicago. A relatively recent convert, she said she was surprised to call women up for compassionate service assignments and have them agree to anything. As she describes it: "I mean, the washing machine is running over, Jeremy is gouging out his brother's eye, her husband left Tuesday with the car payment and hasn't been back, and she's caroling, 'Why, I'd be happy to take a casserole over to Susi.' Because I'm the Relief Society president, right? Now, before I ask anybody to do anything, I kind of visit and find out where they are in their lives and what's going on — to see if maybe they need some help before I start asking them to help someone else."

Informed obedience is obviously time consuming. It will probably never be very popular with highly bureaucratized organizations if they have a choice, because it replaces a focus on rapid and efficient task performance by basically interchangeable workers with a focus on understanding and owning the process. This means that leaders cannot simply concentrate on end products but must spend a great deal of time promoting the process of understanding, allowing experimentation and even mistakes, and honoring the process itself as important. My mission president once said that he felt his primary purpose was to send every missionary home with a testimony; convert baptisms were secondary. He had based this decision on appraising the results of previous mission presidents whose emphasis had been on the baptisms, but it meant that he was sometimes seen as out of step by his own superiors. Convert baptisms are quick and easy to count. The faith of a returned missionary who goes back to raise her five children to be spiritually healthy and happy or to serve as a sensitive and loving elders' quorum president can be fully appraised only years later and then usually indirectly. Then, too, many people who are asked for reasons and information when they have asked for obedience become frustrated and impatient. "It would be so simple just to do it and get it over with rather than carp and niggle," they think. "And besides that I don't know the reasons myself."

If we make due allowances for the limitations of our own point of view and accept the built-in conflicts involving obedience which come with any organization, we still need to decide what to do about it. Prompt, unprocessed obedience is probably not possible for intellectuals on a very wide range of issues, because it counters their personality and training. For that reason, informed obedience is a much better operational strategy. Still I think a much more worthwhile goal is mature obedience, consecrated obedience.

I like to hear children sing, "I Am a Child of God." I don't like to hear adults sing it. I'm sorry it's in the new hymnal. *Everybody's* a child of God. All you have to do to be a child of God is to be born. Big deal. The hard part is to become an adult of God. Most of us get stuck in being an adolescent of God. We whine. We sulk. We have spurts of devotion and conformity followed by either rebellion or terminal sloth. We are dependent, frightened, arrogant, insecure. We want someone to tell us what to do and get mad when they do.

The adolescent model is, it seems to me, instructive for another reason. Jean Baker Miller's psychological work attacks the whole way we have viewed the task of growing up for the past hundred years. For me the parallels with becoming spirit adults are inescapable.

According to a summary of Miller's work, "From Erik Erikson to Daniel Levinson, psychological models of human development posit that the truly well integrated and functioning human being is the person who has 'gone through a series of painful crises by which the individual accomplishes a sequence of allegedly essential separations from others and thereby achieves an inner sense of separated individuation. [Finally] when the individual arrives at the stage called "Intimacy," he is supposed to be able to be intimate with another person(s), having spent all of his prior development geared to something very different.'

"In Daniel Levinson's *The Seasons of a Man's Life*, men are first supposed to move away from their mother and then, gradually, from everyone else. If they have a mentor, for example, at some point—in their thirties—they're supposed to break away from him. He calls this 'becoming your own man.' Of course, about ten years later, this 'independent man' has a midlife crisis, and Levinson never asks why."

Miller denies that a sense of self develops through differentiation. Instead, she argues, we pass through a "stage of development she calls 'agency in community.'" If, as she asserts, "children develop because of their positive relationship to a caretaker, then they develop not a separate sense of self, but rather a more complex sense of self that becomes defined and refined as they enter into ever more complex relationships with others" (in "Anger, Power and Women's Sense of Self," *Ms.*, July 1985, 42-45).

Much of what I term adolescent behavior between people like us and the church we love/hate seems an attempt at differentiation through separation, the classic adolescent crisis. This process nearly always involves disobedience ("I'll show you. You can't tell me what to do.") and nearly always involves pain. Pain has limited utility. I think that the circumstances which produce growth are very often and perhaps inevitably painful, but my own experience has been that growth itself is intensely pleasurable — even joyful. There is, in short, no virtue in making things difficult on purpose.

Thus I wonder if our painful resistance to what we perceive as oppression in the church can sometimes be the wrongheaded working out of the wrong model, of the individuation-through-differentiation model. This model produces alienation and a lessened capacity for intimate experiences, including, I believe, a lessened capacity for intimate experiences with the Savior and the Holy Ghost. I wonder if a more fruitful path might be the model proposed by Miller, that of "agency in community," where we acquire a more complex sense of self.

In my own life, I am struggling with an image of what consecrated obedience might be, trying to understand what the Lord in love is asking me to offer him in my whole life. Part of that life, that love, and that obedience is expressed through the church. The church shapes and colors my religious life, but it does not wholly comprise my religious life, nor does it determine the quality of my religious life. Obedience to the church is not just a me-versus-them issue but one element in a much larger and very dynamic relationship.

Mature obedience, I feel, has to be motivated by love not fear. It has to be deeply rooted in a testimony of the redemptive sacrifice of the Savior and a profoundly personal knowledge that he loves and values me — not my brilliant intellect, not any of the particular roles I might play, but the core-me. It is not an exchange of responsibilities and duties but the interplay, complexity, and richness of an ongoing, intimate, powerful relationship.

The questions still remain. Should we obey? Of course. But whom? and how? and when? Is disobedience justified? Of course. But to whom? and to what? and when? In hammering out answers to those questions on a daily basis within our own families, wards, and stakes, we exercise our "agency in community" and in fact find that we *are* agents within our community. To offer someone—whether the Lord or another fallible mortal like ourselves—blind, reflexive obedience is a terrible gift that can only be asked for in ignorance and given in abdication of self. To offer someone informed obedience is the act of a responsible agent, but it can produce an adversarial relationship that becomes spiritually sterile if the demands for information exceed the ability of the community to provide them— with loss to both.

To offer mature obedience is an act of loving responsibility in a dynamic where the primary tension lies not between the individual and the community but between the individual and the Lord. To someone holding out for fully informed obedience, mature obedience may look blind because part of the information it accepts will not be rational. To someone who wants prompt obedience, mature obedience may even look like disobedience since it will be based on principle rather than programs and practices.

If this seems ambiguous that's because it is. Growing up spiritually is an ambiguous process. It requires accepting ambiguity. But I know of no other process that gives us power in proportion only as our love increases so that we can use power worthily. And we should never ask an organization to do our growing up for us.

3.
The Two Churches of Mormonism

Ron Molen

THE WARD, THE LOVING COMMUNITY AT THE CENTER OF MORMON religious life, is the final destination of Mormonism, the place where the most important things happen. It is the most dynamic of church institutions, the community shared equally by leaders and members alike. But the ward as a community of the faithful has become less ambitious, less important. This process of reductionism could have threatening consequences.

The social contract is the basis for any community. It is a natural consensus, an agreement, between those who lead and those who follow, those who make policy and those who respond. It is a recognition of what Rousseau refers to as the general will, the will of the majority. In a democracy, monarchy, and theocracy, certain rules hold. Those who lead must recognize the needs, desires, and hopes of those who follow; those who follow must assume the responsibilities of good and loyal citizens. This natural sovereignty and territorial right must be respected by presidents, kings, and authorities. Revolutions result when leaders disregard the fundamental needs and inherent rights of their followers.

How then does the social contract relate to the church? In the Mormon tradition, the General Authorities and the large managing bureaucracy constitute the central church and rule the organization as a whole. I will refer to this entity as *management*, that part of the church which leads, manages, provides a service. The membership at large comprises the other church, the church which follows. I call this church experienced at the ward level the *community*. These two churches sometimes have conflicting goals and needs. But there are natural boundaries and natural territories which ought to be respected. Only the social contract can insure a balancing, and thus a proper functioning, of the church.

Unfortunately the needs of management are consistently met, while the needs of the community remain unclear, undefined, disregarded. The social contract is out of balance. A condition exists similar to that which caused early Americans to complain about "taxation without representation." The natural rights of the community have been violated by management. All the power and wealth belong to management. Obedience is demanded from the local church with few demonstrable benefits following.

This imbalance does not result because those in the hierarchy have despotic motives but rather because they see themselves as chosen leaders and are awed by the responsibility. The control by management has evolved slowly. The challenge of rapid growth, the problems of managing diverse peoples, a concern that the religious expression remain simple, and a commitment to financial stability have all played a part in decisions which have slowly and methodically concentrated power. Despite noble motives, a rigid, centrist form evolved; with no representation from the community. Management simply got its way.

We are not talking about theological matters defined by revelation but rather procedures required of a new, large institution. Of course guidelines had to be established, methods and systems put into place. But are all these methods and systems positive? Do the procedures of management benefit the community? Even more fundamental, do they conflict with the restored gospel—with free agency, with the view that the glory of God is intelligence, with the concept of eternal progress, and with the optimism of the ideal which counters Calvinism: "man is that he might have joy?"

All of these concepts are of enormous importance to members within the community but seem to get in the way of the procedures of management. Demeaning alternatives are often promoted, undoubtedly to make management easier for a remote and too often isolated leadership. Obedience is emphasized; free agency is often disregarded. Correlation is emphasized; individual intelligence is minimized. Repetitive activities such as church attendance, missionary work, temple attendance are stressed with few alternatives for the individual to move beyond repetition. Eternal progress remains a remote ideal. The organized religious experience has become so efficient, so minimal, there is little cause for celebration, and the joy which should result from intelligent, righteous living remains unrealized. The free and open aspirations of the faithful are subordinated, even crushed, by the demands of institutional conformity. The natural balance is disregarded, the community territory violated. Simplistic phrases and formulas (such as the "Forever Family") replace the challenge to the individual of the restored truths, the truths which once set us apart from conventional Christianity.

Such criticisms are not made to just censure but rather to establish the basis for the following questions: (1) Why do we need an all-powerful management? (2) At what distance is revelation and even inspiration still relevant? (3) Is the main responsibility of management to serve or to rule the community? (4) How would the church be different if management existed primarily to serve the community? (5) Is there a natural territory for management and for the community? (6) What would be the basis, that point of balance, for an authentic social contract between management and community?

In order to begin answering these question, it is necessary to first consider the limitations inherent in total domination by management.

First limitation: The rejection of two-way communication.

Although there is a continual flow of information from management, the community has no legitimate vehicle for responding. Obedience to encyclicals is not expected but demanded. Curiosity concerning how various programs are working is minimal if it exists at all. Here, of course, is a clearly visible imbalance — a total disinterest in the general will demonstrated by management.

Second limitation: The office and calling of a stake president.

In every sense, the stake president is the local representative of management. He is chosen by management because he is a man to be trusted. His popularity with the community is of secondary importance. Often the stake president has aspirations in management. As a result he seldom reports problems with various programs. Here is a clear violation of community sovereignty, a disregard for the general will.

Third limitation: Division of the priesthood.

Management priesthood, which includes the authorities as well as the bureaucracy, has social, economic, and spiritual power over the church. The bureaucrats, a paid ministry if you will, have power over bishops, even stake presidents. The priesthood of the community is limited to spiritual powers—a clear violation of natural sovereignty.

Fourth limitation: The total financial power of management.

Tithing money from wards across the nation arrives at the church bank Sunday evening, a very efficient system to insure control from the top. A typical ward generates over $100,000 per year in tithing alone, and a typical stake can account for $1,000,000 per year. When a new ward building is built (remember three wards) and management provides the money for a new $1,000,000 building, it is hardly magnanimous since the stake donates that amount annually.

Fifth limitation: Management's control of all charitable donations and limiting these donations to church-sponsored programs.

Although the welfare plan is a highly esteemed program, it assists no more than 2 percent of the church membership. The community is rarely if ever allowed to join with other denominations in funding the critical charitable needs of the cities and towns where the wards are located. Since it makes no contribution and remains socially aloof, a Mormon ward is not a respected institution in many local communities.

Sixth limitation: Management's resorting to various forms of coercion, often centered around the collection of tithes.

By decree of management, marriage for eternity must occur in the temple. (Again tithing is a requirement for a recommend.) There attendance for both participants and guests is restricted to full tithe payers. Another example: temples are built throughout the world so that members will not have an excuse to be without a recommend. Management is well aware that where temples are built, tithing increases.

Management insists that confession to the bishop is required before repentance can be fully accepted. Excommunication is the result if the sin is thought to be grave enough. Personal behavior is thereby made public, institutional values are made supreme, and the obsession with personal transgression can poison the community with unfounded suspicion and gossip.

The missionary program is another example of social coercion. Management allows no legitimate alternative for a healthy, faithful nineteen-year-old male. Despite this only 32 percent participate, and 68 percent are left wanting.

Seventh limitation: The reduction of the basic church program to three hours of worship on Sunday.

There is little or no concern whether this format is beneficial to the optimum functioning of the community. This marathon of meetings is questionable even for adults, and for children it is often a disaster. Behavior modification is based on a system of rewards. The rewards of three hours of sitting for children are non-existent and the negative reinforcement so pervasive that one must question how our children will respond to the church once they are free to choose for themselves. Statistical data indicating that only about 50 percent of the members of an average ward choose to participate suggests we already have a problem.

Eighth limitation: The importance to management of institutional perpetuation.

The mindless defense of a sacred history, even the fear of history itself, is pervasive. Anything which could tarnish an over-polished image is disdained.

Ninth limitation: A new fundamentalism, even a neo-Calvinism, requiring a tightening of theological positions and a rigidifying of form.

This is the response of a management struggling to control and fearful of what might result if that control was lost. The creation of a vast bureaucracy, trusted more than the community, is used, often with disregard, to keep the community in line. Management bureaucracy controls everything from teaching manuals to architecture and music. The results are predictable, banal, nothing worthy of praise.

The previous discussion of the limitations resulting from total control of management provides the basis for a most important consideration. How would the church be different if management served the community? What if the community assumed its natural sovereignty, its inherent powers, functions, purposes? What could be anticipated if a new balance were struck, an authentic social contract achieved? Of course this is little more than wishful think-

ing, yet it is necessary if we are to clarify the great untapped potential of the community.

First, we would expect that two-way communication would
be established, a recognition and acceptance of the general will.
Change can only begin to occur when management is made aware
of the many flaws in methods and procedures. In order to make
intelligent recommendations, experimentation by the community
would be required. Reporting the results to management could be
extremely helpful. An important function of management would be
to dispense this information, still recognizing that there are many
ways to celebrate the gospel. Each community would then have the
right to determine what programs and systems worked best for it.
A rich diversity and vitality would result.

The main purpose of local initiative would be to create an
optimum environment for rearing the young, an environment
where the individual was encouraged, respected, loved, where the
community was there to assist not dominate, where a positive self-
image was accessible for all and considered of more value than a
guilt-driven testimony. Success of the community would be determined by the success of the individuals comprising it.

Second, the stake president would be chosen by both management and the community. This would be imperative to establish a
trust, an intelligent working relationship between management and
community. In the process the stake organization would achieve a
new relevance.

Third, there is one priesthood, and the community would
have to achieve equality with management. This means equal social,
economic, and spiritual powers. Management bureaucracy would of
necessity shrink in size because it no longer was required to dominate the community but rather assist.

Fourth, since women make an enormous contribution to the
proper functioning of the community, limitation of priesthood to a
single gender would cease. Women would become full participants
in a lay priesthood that needs their vitality.

Fifth, the community would have the financial muscle to
solve its own needs. It would achieve financial independence. Management would also have the financial capacity to support its vital
functions. In simple terms, all the tithing would not go to management, but the majority would remain in the community, as it did

until the turn of the century, to invest in significant local programs and needs.

Sixth, the community would assume its charitable responsibilities in the towns and cities in which it exists. Relief Society and priesthood programs would become less institutional, less myopic, and would reach out into the community to participate in solving community needs. Housing for the aged, recreational facilities, and programs for the youth, even communal experiments in food production and other forms of self-sufficiency, could be functioning programs.

Seventh, the community would perform the primary proselyting function, not through an exotic marketing program but rather in simply being available to those interested in joining a vital socioreligious experiment. The entire strategy would be based on the premise that if the product is good enough, people will want to become part of it. The problem as it exists today, with 80 percent of the converts falling away because they are not integrated into the community, would be resolved.

Eight, church attendance would become enjoyable. Meetings would be shortened, refreshments served, camaraderie encouraged. Rewards for participation in the community would be prevalent. Members would get to know each other well. An authenticity of community would be achieved.

Ninth, theology would be opened to investigation. History would be analyzed, truth sought. A real, authentic, verifiable heritage would be established and with this new found integrity could be built upon. A rich pluralism would develop, even a regional expression. The church in South America would no longer replicate the church in Utah.

Tenth, church buildings would be designed by those who use the space not reproduced by a remote bureaucracy. The vitality, the creative ingenuity of the members would be expressed in every facet of the building. The quality of the architecture would reflect the quality of the community. We have a responsibility as a church wherever we go to honor the people, the land, their traditions, their hopes and aspirations. Perhaps in Guatemala the members could attend church in some simple indigenous structure which honored and respected their way of life rather than reproducing the standard plan.

Recently a worker on the General Motors production line was asked by a research specialist if anyone in management had ever asked for suggestions on how to better perform his specific task. He replied that he had many suggestions but that in his thirty years with the company no one had ever asked. Even attempts to make recommendations were instantly rejected. It is a classic example of what is backward and reactionary about contemporary American industry, and the same could be said of church management. It is disinterested in how programs, methods, activities, and life in the community could be improved.

The community needs the space, the freedom to solve its own particular problems using the talents and capabilities of its members. Programs should be user-designed. Goals and parameters could be set by management, but their accomplishment should be left to local initiative. Management could recommend some systems over others, but it should no longer establish a single solution for everyone, everywhere, for everything.

In summary:

We do not need an all-powerful management. We need leadership with the tolerance and wisdom to recognize the great diversity of people and ideas.

We do not need a single, universal system for practicing the faith, because that system must eventually stagnate as in fact it already has.

The main function of management is to assist the community not to dominate it.

Life in the community would improve immeasurably, and a higher percentage of activity could be expected if the community could respond directly to the needs of its members.

Management will have to understand and show deference to the general will.

A social contract, a point of balance between management and community, must be achieved if the church is to succeed in the future.

Management must not treat the community differentially. The church in South America must develop its own resources for survival. A subsidized community is not a real community. A real community must have the internal capacity to survive on its own. Management should not take critical funding from one community and give to another without the consent of the donating community.

The two churches of Mormonism must find a new balance, a respect for natural sovereignty, a new social contract in order to provide intelligent, workable, common sense solutions to the needs of its members. Management must learn to accept its limitations; the community must learn to assume its full responsibilities. That point of balance where an authentic social contract is achieved is impossible to fix and will forever be so. Yet we are presently a great distance away. But if we were to approach that point, we would recognize it.

We would realize that if a ward is to achieve community, it must be given the right to experiment, make mistakes, discover a better way, establish its credentials, prove its validity, demonstrate that through righteous principles people can in fact rule themselves.

Most of all, life in the ward should not be dull, repetitive, mind-numbing. It should be joyful, hopeful, purposeful, filled with fresh air and sunlight. Obedience, correlation, repetition pave the way to a corporate sterility. Free agency, the glory of God is intelligence, eternal progress, man is that he might have joy—all remain valid stepping stones. The Kingdom of God in a Promised Land can never be achieved by a remote leadership directing a bureaucracy. It will be achieved by an intelligent, righteous people with the common sense to see what needs to be done and the love and energy to accomplish it.

4.
The Better for My Foes:
The Role of Opposition

Elouise M. Bell

I DRAW MY INSPIRATION FROM TWO SOURCES – THE NOTED American political philosopher and journalist Walter Lippmann and the clown or fool from Shakespeare's *Twelfth Night*. Since clowning is the older and in some ways more serious profession, let us begin there.

As you remember, the fools in Shakespeare's dramas are anything but fools. Often the greatest wisdom of a play comes from that quarter. The clown in *Twelfth Night* is no exception. In Act V, scene 1, Orsino, the duke of Illyria, says to the clown by way of greeting, "How dost thou, my good fellow?"

The clown replies, "Truly, sir, the better for my foes and the worse for my friends."

The duke tries to correct him: "Just the contrary—the better for thy friends."

"No sir, the worse."

"How can that be?"

"Marry, sir, they praise me and make an ass of me. Now my foes tell me plainly I am an ass, so that by my foes, sir, I profit in the knowledge of myself, and by my friends I am abused. So that . . . the worse for my friends, and the better for my foes."

To which the duke replies. "Why this is excellent." Which, I hope to establish, it is indeed.

The same insight came to King Lear after he had been so reduced in circumstances that he was literally naked and homeless upon the moor in a raging storm. Speaking in anger and bitterness about the many lackeys and paid flatterers who had clustered around him in his former days of glory, he said, "They told me I was ague-proof." That is, they flattered him so outrageously that he believed he was immune even from the common afflictions such as ague or flu, which are the lot of humankind.

Thus Lear is pointing out that sometimes those who agree easily and quickly with us do us a disservice. And the clown is explaining that those whom we may *consider* our foes can actually be our greatest benefactors.

The concept of valued opposition is not, I fear, very well understood in Mormon culture. And without it we cause ourselves and others needless grief and may actually hinder what we would advance. As I have listened to speeches and public discussions, read letters to the editors of several newspapers both in Utah and outside, heard people debate among themselves on various controversies—ranging from the activities of the Environmental Protection Agency to the merits of a constitutional amendment on equal rights—I have observed four general attitudes, four ways of viewing opposition. There are surely others, but these four seem to predominate: (1) opposition as persecution, (2) opposition as counsel for the defense, (3) opposition as airing of personal opinion, and (4) opposition as sand in the shoes.

The first attitude reveals what we could call a Hatfield-McCoy pattern of response, a "Them 'n Us" philosophy, whose motto is, "Fire at Will, For the Enemy Is All Around Us!" This philosophy teaches that the opposition is basically a passel of no-good skunks out to get Us in every way possible and that even though this week our concern may be with stopping them from stealing our hogs, we can never let our guard down. Next week They (or someone in cahoots with Them) will be trying to poison the well or dynamite the privy. In other words this camp views the opposition as unmitigated evil, and as far as *listening* to the opposition goes, they listen only long enough to fix the enemy position before blasting away.

(When I originally formulated these ideas, I wrote, "I really don't think this militia group to be very large, but they are loud." Today I feel a deeper concern. The ranks of the self-appointed righteous seem to be swelling, if not yet a majority.)

For Mormons and for many other Christians, the problem arises, I believe, out of the confusion of human opposition—in matters political, economic, educational, even religious—with the supernatural. It is understandably easy but unequivocally dangerous to move from viewing Satan as the opposition to viewing any mortal opposition as satanic. To put it another way, all that is of Satan is opposition, but all that opposes us is not satanic. Yet down through the centuries, such an attitude has often prevailed as men have made the slippery step from "This is what we believe" to "This is what *God* believes, and death to the infidels who believe otherwise."

Not every skirmish is a holy war. We can effectively root out waste and inefficiency in public office without believing that every politician is in the pay of Satan. We can debate how our communities and valleys can best be developed and protected without convincing ourselves and others that those who oppose us (on whatever side they happen to be) are advance men for the adversary. We can consider how best to structure our schools without consigning the neighbor who disagrees with us to the legions of Lucifer.

Now to the second attitude toward opposition. This is in many respects a more intelligent approach to opposition, so much so in fact that I'm going to call it the lawyer's attitude. But intelligent as this attitude is in the right place, it is still not the appropriate stance for people trying seriously to discover how best to regulate our government, outfit our schools, develop our resources, and incorporate a moral ethic into our society.

This attitude toward opposition says, "We must listen to the opposition, study them closely, read their literature, and hear their spokespersons, in order that we may know how to refute their arguments." I call this the lawyer's attitude because the lawyer does not go into court to tell all she knows of a case, and certainly she does not go into court to learn what she does not know. In fact an old axiom says that a lawyer must never ask of a witness any question to which she, the lawyer, does not already know the answer. There must be, in short, no surprises. The lawyer is in court, is being paid, to advocate one particular position with all the skill and eloquence she has. She must try to outwit her opponents by guessing what form their questioning will take. She must try to know about any evidence they plan to introduce, any witness they may call. She tries to think of every point the opposing lawyers could conceivably make—not so that she can change her mind about what she believes but so that she will be prepared in court for any direction the argument may take.

Given the nature of our judicial system, such an attitude is professionally justified. One or more lawyers represent each side of a case, and the judge and jury decide the truth as best they can. But the individual truth seeker who has the lawyer's attitude about the opposition is shortchanging himself. Who will be the judge if he has already made up his mind before he hears what the other side has to say, if he listens only to refute? Such a person has skipped a crucial step.

The third attitude is related to the second in that it allows all opponents "their day in court." This attitude — and I have heard it widely voiced in the church — says, "You are entitled to your own opinion, but this is what I believe" (implying, "And I don't intend to change"). What could be fairer than that? Well, fair it may be, but foolish it certainly is. Remember Shakespeare's fool? He did not merely allow his foes to talk. He listened to them and was ready to change his views on the basis of what they said if it was logical and valid. Yet many of us today think of ourselves as enlightened because we are willing to "let others have their say" without seriously considering their say. The danger of this approach is brilliantly explained by the great essayist Walter Lippmann in an article entitled "The Indispensable Opposition" (August 1939, *The Atlantic Monthly*). In this essay Lippmann is discussing why it is so important to protect the right of free speech:

"We take, it seems to me, a naively self-righteous view when we argue as if the right of our opponents to speak were something that we protect because we are magnanimous, noble, and unselfish. The compelling reason . . . is that we must protect the right of our opponents to speak because we must hear what they have to say.

"This is the creative principle of freedom of speech, not that it is a system for the tolerating of error, but that it is a system for finding the truth. . . . And so, if we truly wish to understand why freedom is necessary in a civilized society, we must begin by realizing that, because freedom of discussion improves our own opinions, the liberties of other men are our own vital necessity. . . .

"The opposition is indispensable. A good statesman, like any other sensible human being, always learns more from his opponents than from his fervent supporters. For his supporters will push him to disaster unless his opponents show him where the dangers are. So if he is wise, he will often pray to be delivered from his friends, because they will ruin him. But, though it hurts, he ought also to pray never to be left without opponents; for they keep him on the path of reason and good sense."

And thus we have returned to the point put forth by the fool. If we are as wise as he, we too will listen to the opposition in order to learn — not merely to fix their positions so we may fire upon them, nor to know their arguments so we may defeat them, nor simply to allow them "equal time" to air their opinions. We will listen to others to learn if our own perceptions are right and true, conscious always that they may not be.

Now there is yet another attitude toward opposition, which is both an attitude and a cause of our problems with opposition generally. I call it the "sand in the shoes" theory. It is related to the "Hatfield-McCoy" school, although proponents are very different in temperament and profoundly different in theology.

The "sand in the shoes" view says that opposition is necessary and inevitable. As we climb the mountain in our great quest, there is bound to be sand in our shoes from time to time. We must simply persevere, patiently removing the sand when it becomes too great an obstruction. Such a philosophy seems eminently sane and courageous, and of course it is, when applied to obstacles such as one's individual crosses — sickness, sorrow, misfortune, what Shakespeare calls "the whips and scorns of time." If that is what one means by opposition, then all is well. But when this philosophy becomes muddied, and opposition broadens to mean "those on the other side" and is considered part of the divinely-decreed testing of one's mettle, then danger sets in. Although the "sand in the shoe" philosopher may be softer spoken than the "persecuted righteous," the roots of their problems are similar — confusing opposition with evil.

And at this point we have come to the quick of the ulcer. For Mormons, opposition has a special meaning, deeply felt if rarely examined, a meaning which grows out of a specific scripture. It is my theory — and I stress that term — that a general misunderstanding of this passage prevails and accounts for our many inappropriate attitudes toward any who line up on the other side of us.

The scripture is found in 2 Nephi 2:11. Father Lehi says to his son Jacob: "For it needs be, that there is an opposition in all things. If not so, my first-born in the wilderness, righteousness could not be brought to pass, neither wickedness, neither holiness nor misery, neither good nor bad. Wherefore, all things must needs be a compound in one; wherefore, if it should be one body it must needs remain as dead, having no life neither death, nor corruption nor incorruption, happiness nor misery, neither sense nor insensibility."

How do we understand this scripture? It seems to me that a great many people interpret it by making two columns — righteousness, holiness, and good on one side (Column A) and wickedness, misery, and bad on the other (Column B). Column B is the opposition, admittedly bad but still necessary so that we might achieve, appreciate, and enjoy Column A, the good things of life.

Lehi, however, says that even *wickedness* could not come to pass, nor misery nor evil, without opposition. If we take the view that the valiant need opposition to build up spiritual muscles, as it were, why would the wicked need it? Do they also need "sand in the shoes" to be tested, to develop character? Notice also that Lehi does not say, "righteousness needs opposition." Though often understood this way, the passage reads differently. Lehi says that it is necessary that there be an opposition in all things. Without that condition as a given, righteousness could not be brought to pass. Righteousness wouldn't even happen in the first place. Quite a different concept.

A few verses on in that same chapter, Lehi speaks of the Lord creating our first parents and the beasts and fowls of the air and then says that after this was done, "It must needs be that there was an opposition; even the forbidden fruit in opposition to the tree of life; the one being sweet and the other bitter" (2 Ne. 2:15). Which fruit was sweet: the fruit of the tree of life or the fruit of the forbidden tree? The word order (plus the additional evidence of Moses 4:12) would suggest it was the forbidden fruit which was sweet and the fruit of the tree of life which was bitter. Is the tree of life, the tree Adam and Eve were encouraged to eat, bad then because it is bitter? Is the bitterness "opposition"? If the tree of life is bitter, must we list it in Column B?

The answer to this question may lie in the earlier verse in the words which explain that "all things must needs be a compound in one." Lehi says, "It must needs be that there is an opposition in all things." Notice *in* all things, not *to*. Could we restate this to say that in all aspects of life there must be and there is a mixture of good and bad, right and wrong, holiness and misery? This mixture, this opposition of qualities, produces a state of constant motion, movement, interchange, growth—of life. Lehi explains, "if it should be one body"—if there were not this compound of qualities—"it must needs remain as dead, having no life neither death."

Consider the possibility (which I believe to be valid) that the "opposition" Lehi speaks of is not in fact the "bad" or "wrong" side of things (Column B) but instead the mixture itself, the intermingling process, the fact that all things in life are a compound. In this sense opposition is not at all a negative circumstance, although it involves negative qualities as well as positive ones. Because we have misinterpreted opposition to mean all the "evils" in Column B, we carry over that connotation to our political, economic, social, environmental, and other debates and consider our human opposition as "evil" or "bad" also—or at least we consider opposing ideas as such. Our misunderstanding of the word has misled us.

In summary of this point then: while I definitely believe we are given struggles and pain and problems in this life in order to strengthen our characters and fortify our souls, to classify our political and other philosophical opposition as part of the "necessary evil" of this life is to accuse them falsely and to martyr ourselves undeservedly.

I offer in conclusion a quotation from LDS president Harold B. Lee: "It is good to be faithful. It is better to be faithful and competent." I believe we will be more competent in our roles as parents, citizens, office holders, and members who would be instrumental in building a Zion society if we thought more deeply and more carefully about the nature of opposition. As a practical start I offer the following suggestions:

1. Beware the impulse to divide opposing camps into Column A and Column B—the good guys and the bad guys. Usually any given political or social stance has both merit and weakness—the "compound in one"—including the view you are proposing.

2. Beware making a person rather than a position the opposition. If we do that we run the risk of losing that person as an ally on another issue about which we both agree. Moreover, if we think of persons as the opposition, we may end up arguing personalities rather than issues, and at that point reason goes out the window.

3. Beware of establishing a predictable pattern of opposition. Emerson taught us that "A foolish consistency is the hobgoblin of little minds." If you can always predict what side of an issue I'm going to be on, that's a sign that I am prejudging, biasing my response, or judging something besides the issues and the arguments.

4. Beware of self-listening to the opposition. This is listening just long enough to decide how you're going to answer, and then not thinking beyond that point.

5. Beware of never changing your mind. I would have very little confidence in a person who had never changed his or her mind on an issue, who had never said, "Well, I thought about that some more; I studied that a bit more deeply, and decided I was wrong."

6. Beware of the passion to take a stand, any stand, now, rather than wait and ponder. Be mature enough and confident enough to be able to live with a few loose ends, a few uncertainties.

7. Beware of confusing God's infallibility with your own. Because the church has access to divine truth, it does not follow that any Mormon who quotes scripture to support his or her view must of necessity be right.

8. Beware abandoning the wisdom of Moroni 10:4, which exhorts us to seek truth with a sincere heart and real intent. If this advice is valid in such a weighty quest as a testimony, surely it is a good model to follow in lesser matters such as political issues. But just as the scripture asks the investigator to seek with real intent, so in temporal matters we must study, which includes listening to our opponents, with truly open minds. The famed historian Marchette Chute has wisely said, "If you know in advance what the truth will be, you will never find it."

The still-young experiment of democracy has had many critics from the days it was first tried in the western world. One of the most oft-repeated objections to government of and by the people is that most people simply do not have the philosophical and rational training and understanding to make wise decisions about government and civic affairs. Most people, according to the nay-sayers, will always be ruled by passion, swayed by prejudice, seduced by propaganda, and hence incapable of enlightened self-government. I do not agree with the nay-sayers. The dangers they warn of are real but not irrevocable. I believe government of and by the people can work. But it can only work when we train ourselves in the principles of

sound thinking, when we are ever mindful of the absolute indispens-
ability of that man or woman across the aisle or on the other side of
the platform, when we, like Shakespeare's wise Fool, know enough to
treasure our "foe," the opposition.

5.
How Much Tolerance Can We Tolerate?

Arthur R. Bassett

SEVERAL YEARS AGO, I TOOK MY FAMILY BACK TO SYRACUSE, NEW York, and began a doctoral program in humanities, centered in American studies. One of my first classes concentrated on the writings of William James, and it was there I experienced one of those turning points in education, affecting one's life forever. One paragraph from a series of lectures James delivered at the Lowell Institute in December 1906 changed forever the way I perceive people. It is from his fourth lecture in which he discusses "The One and the Many," different ways of approaching life:

"In this present hour I wish to . . . [focus] upon the ancient problem of 'the one and the many.' I suspect that in but few of you has this problem occasioned sleepless nights, and I should not be astonished if some of you told me it had never vexed you at all. I myself have come, by long brooding over it, to consider it the most central of all philosophic problems, central because so pregnant. I mean by this that if you know whether a man is a decided monist or a decided pluralist, you perhaps know more about the rest of his opinions than if you give him any other name ending in *-ist*. To believe in the one or in the many, that is the classification with the maximum number of consequences. So bear with me for an hour while I try to inspire you with my own interest in this problem."[1]

James uses the terms monism and pluralism, which are philosophical terms with cosmological implications. I suspect that if he had been a political scientist instead, he might have used the

terms conservative and liberal, which can popularly be applied
about the same way. James was a devout pluralist himself.

If his observation is right, and I am convinced that it is, this
means that the best index to a person's character is found in his or
her ability to tolerate a variety of differing ideas and life styles. The
question I would have us consider then is: How much tolerance can
we tolerate—both as individuals and as a people? And by extension
the more difficult question: How much pluralism *should* we tolerate
and encourage?

I have no answer to these questions, but I do wonder about
them often. I confess that I am basically a pluralist by conviction and
am increasingly becoming so by temperament. I find stimulation
and insight (as well as frustration) in viewpoints different from my
own, especially within the church context. My present concern
stems from the fact that I sense I am a pluralist in a church whose
membership is largely oriented toward monism.

As a people we have achieved a remarkable degree of homogeneity during the last century and a half. No one who has lived
among us and been aware of our activities can doubt this. Some have
suggested (though I am not prepared to agree without strong reser-
vations) that we demonstrate a striking similarity even in our artistic
and political views, in our dress, our thoughts, and our general
demeanor.

Whether these observations are accurate or not, it is true
that we pride ourselves as a people that on any given Sunday any-
where in the world, we can drop in on a Mormon meeting and feel as
if we were in our home ward. The correlation program has unified to
an amazing degree the things we will talk about and the way we
will talk about them. Not only are we told what we should discuss but
(if one reads the teachers' manuals) also the conclusions that we
should reach. The sermons we hear will be noticeably similar both in
content and style. And unless one is treated to the refreshing dissim-
ilarity of the prayer of a new convert, the prayers will sound very
much alike, especially the sacramental prayers (though we do not
use chants in the manner of the Catholic church, the uniformity of
rhythm, intonation, inflection, and accented words used in the sacrament prayer by our young priests throughout the world has always
intrigued me).

Part of this is as it should be. No one would dispute that unity is one of the major themes (if not the dominant theme) of scripture. The essence of the gospel is found in a single word: *atonement*. The gospel is literally the news of Christ's providing the way for us to be bonded together in love: with our Father in Heaven, with each other, and with ourselves. Atonement is a proper synonym for love. It is at the core of everything the church should represent.

Its antithesis—lack of unity—has been destructive to society at all levels. That seems to be the message of the confusion of tongues at the tower of Babel, a confusion perpetuated through the image of Israel's enemy, Babylon (which has its etymological origins in the Hebrew word for confusion). This Old Testament event has its healing counterpart in the New Testament experience at Pentecost, where such confusion of tongues was suspended, at least momen-tarily, in Jerusalem.

On the personal level, if I may alter Paul's famous passage slightly, the wages of sin prove to be alienation—estrangement from God, from self, or from others. I have found separation from those who matter most to be among the most unbearable of all punish-ments, among the most excruciating causes of suffering. Atonement binds and brings strength and comfort in troubled times; alienation divides and takes away all sense of worth and well-being.

The scriptures are filled with exhortations on unity. Zion was called Zion "because they were of one heart and one mind" (Moses 7:18). John in his Gospel stresses continually the unity between Jesus and his father: "I and my father are one" echoes throughout (John 10:30). And while presenting his final petition to God before his struggles in Gethsemane and Golgotha, the Master prayed that his disciples would reflect the same sense of solidarity (17:20).

This unchanging theme dominates the epistles of Paul. The Corinthians are chastised for the petty divisions that are beginning to appear among them (1 Cor. 1:10). The Ephesians are admonished to remember that there is "one body, and one Spirit, . . . one hope of [their] calling; one Lord, one faith, one baptism, one God and Father of all, who is above all, and through all, and in [them] all" (Eph. 4:4). In our own day the theme is echoed in the LDS Doctrine and Covenants: "Be one" becomes the admonition of the Lord to the Saints in Fayette, New York, who were neglecting their poor, "and if ye are not one, ye are not mine" (38:27).

Many positive consequences stem from unity. It brings with it a sense of familiarity, of safety and certainty, of belonging, and of personal worth—all of which further contribute to a sense of security and well-being. These empower us to persevere and to move comfortably without fear over the face of the entire planet, at least among our own. Any of us who have traveled to any extent can testify to the truthfulness of this. We literally are "no more strangers and foreigners, but fellow citizens with the saints" everywhere in the world (Eph. 2:19).

That, however, is the "good news" of the gospel. There is also a potentially dark side to the same stance, especially if we are not alert to the destructive potential of this other extreme. Those who have unbalanced preferences for religious monism, like the Pharisees of biblical fame, can demonstrate tendencies toward at least two shortcomings: xenophobia, a fear or hatred of those unlike themselves; and homogeneity, an unhealthy obsession with the need for conformity, usually to their own way of thinking and performing.

One mode of unity can produce anti-Christian elitism. It should be obvious from past performances of the covenant people (such as ancient Israel, especially the Pharisees) that strongly unified groups easily fall prey to a posture of exclusion rather than one of inclusion. In my view this stance is antithetical to the mission and message of the Savior.

We all like to be thought of as being special and exclusive. It sets us apart as distinct. It does nice things for our ego. We enjoy owning and driving exclusive cars, living in exclusive neighborhoods, joining exclusive clubs, wearing exclusive clothes. The word itself has a nice "yuppie" ring about it. It carries with it a sense of being better than others. It says *important*. But at its roots it simply says exclusion, the omission of others. And this connotation somehow seems out of sync with the cherished American ideal of democracy and the Christian concept of brotherhood.

Certainly it seems out of sync with the message which the Savior brought of love and concern for others. One of the things that his disciples and enemies alike had a difficult time understanding was his inclusiveness: publicans, harlots, and wine-drinkers, Samaritan women, lepers, women taken in adultery, troublesome parents pressing for a blessing for their children, calloused soldiers nailing him to a cross—and many others that the orthodox Pharisaic leaders of the Jewish sects (and often even his own disciples) excluded from their fellowship. The Savior reached out with concern to all of them and included them as much as they would allow him. Inclusion was at the core of his good news; exclusion was opposed to his concept of love.

In the LDS church we sometimes unwittingly do a rather effective job of fostering xenophobia, especially with our youth, isolating the members mentally and socially from those outside the faith. The multiplication of meetings and other demands on their time is only one means of doing this. (Although I appreciate — more than I can express — the time volunteered in behalf of my children by caring individuals in my ward, I for one have a difficult time understanding the thinking that suggests that the answer to drug addiction, sexual promiscuity, and other problems is to institute more activities for the youth during the week.) Second, our youth are constantly taught, both at church and at home, how much better they are than those outside of the faith (or even those of earlier generations) and how what they are doing is more important than what others are doing.

We inadvertently fill their thinking with militaristic metaphors common in our teachings: they are a royal army, putting on the armor of God, warring against the forces of evil. It seemed to me when I was growing up that we were eternally at war with someone or something and that the adoption of a military mentality was crucial to my survival. Those outside of the church had driven and killed my ancestors, and it was only a matter of time before they would be at it again. Over and over this warfare was presented as one of the conditions of the last days — for which days I had been preserved in heaven.

The attitude of "us-versus-them" underlies the principle of scapegoating. Every group seems to function best with a scapegoat to unite against in order to survive or to acquire a sense of worth: the unkept, smelly, awkward boy in the kindergarten class; the girl who wants too much to be popular in the high school; the rival high school or college; the other ward with the "dirty players" on its basketball team; the competition in business; the foreign nation, especially if it currently carries a tinge of socialism.

We are constantly on the attack against someone or something. We love to unite against them. We love to hate them and to feel superior to them. We do it almost instinctively. And within the church it concerns me that the hatred we teach against Lucifer (and the forces of evil) is so easily transferred into hatred of those whose ideas are different from our own in any way. Isolated from others in such a manner, how can we possibly reach out to share those things that we have come as a people to cherish? Such a stance seems detrimental to the entire concept of missionary work. But equally important, how can we glean rich insights about life from others if we draw back exclusively into our own society?

Unfortunately, our desire for unity and exclusivity can encourage a smugness about our own endeavors and accomplishments and a degree of apathy or even intolerance toward that which "the world" is doing: civil rights marches, peace movements, poverty programs, artistic and scholarly endeavors. Time devoted to such interests is time away from the meetings and other obligations we try to equate with the building of the kingdom of God. That which WE are doing is infinitely more significant than that which THEY are doing—or thinking. That which WE have is far superior in every way to that which THEY have.

I was intrigued a few years ago by the account of one of my close friends, who is an estate planner. In the course of his business, he met a non-Mormon physician who had moved into the inner city of Salt Lake, where he lived and worked with the poor. After a time this doctor and his wife decided to take their two children on a long-overdue vacation. At a rest stop the couple watched in horror as their children, hand in hand, were hit and killed by a truck. After the funeral the couple decided to go to India and volunteer their services to one of the programs there to help build better communities. I will never forget the frustration of my Mormon friend, and more especially his wife, as they later tried to teach the couple the principles and ordinances of Mormonism as the doctor simultaneously tried to convince my friend that he should become involved in contributing to the work in India. My friend was forced to wrestle anew with the issue of who was the better Christian.

I wonder what our church would be like today if its founder had not been moved by the Second Great Awakening, if there had not been temperance societies in Kirtland, Ohio, if some of the Saints there had not followed a practice of having all things in common prior to Joseph Smith's arrival, or if the social gospel movement of the late nineteenth century had not raised vital issues which church leaders also tried to address. Having taught American religions for some time, I am often pained by the apathy—and sometimes antagonism—some students display when the religious beliefs of others are discussed. "We have the truth," their boredom testifies, "and what do we possibly have to learn from the beliefs of others, from the philosophies of men?"

At such times I find encouragement in some of the comments of Joseph Smith: "I love that man better who swears a stream as long as my arm yet deals justice to his neighbors and mercifully deals his substance to the poor, than the long, smoothfaced hypocrite"[2] or "Friendship is one of the grand fundamental principles of "Mormonism"; [it is designed] to revolutionize and civilize the world, and cause wars and contentions to cease and men to become friends and brothers."[3] Further, Joseph noted, it is through these friendships and sharing, often with those outside of the faith, that we come to some of those important insights in this life that make us what he called "true Mormons": "Have the Presbyterians any truth? Yes. Have the Baptists, Methodists, etc., any truth? Yes. They all have a little truth mixed with error. We should gather all the good and true principles in the world and treasure them up, or we shall not come out true 'Mormons.' "[4]

Brigham Young echoed something of the same idea: "Some who call themselves Christians are very tenacious with regard to the Universalians, yet the latter possess many excellent ideas and truths. Have the Catholics? Yes, a great many very excellent truths. Have the Protestants? Yes, from first to last. Has the infidel? Yes, he has a good deal of truth; and truth is all over the earth. . . . Do you think there is any truth in hell? Yes, a great deal, and where truth is there we calculate the Lord has a right to be."[5]

While I was doing graduate work, which involved a number of classes in philosophy (such as existed at BYU in those days), I was often confronted by friends and relatives with raised eyebrows and the question: "What are you studying *that* for?" After going through this catechism repeatedly, I finally found a satisfying response: "I am discovering that philosophy has the questions and the gospel has the answers, and I am finding one almost meaningless without the other." For example, I never appreciated Paul's triad of faith, hope, and charity so well as I did after studying existentialism, with its emphasis on absurdity, despair, and alienation. I never found the scriptures as poignant and powerful as I did after studying the faith of others, both believers and atheists.

I suspect that none of us fully comprehends ourselves — what we believe and what we stand for — until we place our intellectual and spiritual values into the market place beside those of others. Even if we end up having to buy back our own from the market, we are richer for the experience. And though obviously there are also important things we learn about ourselves in isolation, I suggest that there are many more things we glean from the diversity in society, both in and out of the church. That is why I have come to opt for a good deal of the spice of plurality along with our unity in the church. I have come to like the idea of including rather than excluding, and I sense that we can all gain by that inclusion.

Plurality or diversity need not be disruptive to unity. In certain respects it appears to me to be an indispensable source of growth and development. Accompanied by tolerance, patience, meekness, gentleness, and some of the other major Christian virtues which go into the larger configuration of love, they seem the very key to an abundant life.

Insistence on conformity is an easier way to maintain unity than persuasion, especially if the authority structure is well established as it is in Mormonism. All parents know this from rearing their children. Give up your ideas, we insist; mine are better. In the process creativity is squelched. That is the tragedy of this approach. And yet we resist the new ideas and insights of those who disagree, and we do it as a matter of common course. I'm sure it would not come as a great shock to those who attend Sunstone symposiums to find that their attendance is a source of discomfort for many within the church. Some people do not like to have their cherished thoughts questioned. We don't like others rocking our boat, especially if we've never learned to swim.

When people in various settings within the church begin to wrestle through the implications of a scripture or a church program, almost inevitably someone will try to short-circuit the discussion by an appeal to authority. This always brings to mind a sentence from Dostoevsky's *The Brothers Karamazov*, in which one of the brothers, a philosopher, relates a story to his brother, a Russian Orthodox priest. The backdrop for the story is the Spanish Inquisition. The

Savior returns, only to be recognized and placed under arrest and thrown into prison by order of the Grand Inquisitor—who later visits Christ in the dungeon. "Did you forget," the Inquisitor queries, "that a tranquil mind or even death is dearer to man than the free choice in the knowledge of good and evil?"

Dostoevsky's words struck responsive chords, both in regard to the lives of others I had known and to my own. Several people I know suffer to some degree from what Walter Kaufmann has aptly termed "decidophobia." There is a certain comfort in having others responsible for important choices in our own lives. That way we win if the decision is right—and we aren't responsible if the decision is wrong. In short we end up winning either way. The trouble is that we lose the growth and insight accompanying the stretching and frustration associated with decision making.

Coupled with this all-too-human tendency to flee responsibility and compounding the problem even further is our recognition that often God requires our obedience, whether we understand or not. The problem is that it is difficult at best to know when God demands our unquestioning obedience and when he wants us to work through a problem on our own, as illustrated in Oliver Cowdery's attempt to translate the Book of Mormon (D&C 9:7-8).

Unfortunately, there are those among us who would like to assume the role of God in controlling the lives of others—unfortunately it is the nature and disposition of *almost all* people to want to exercise unrighteous dominion over the souls of men and women (D&C 121:39). Frequently that desire for dominion is not even the consequence of evil designs (to use the terminology of the Doctrine and Covenants). Sometimes, as with parents, the desire is the result of frustration or lack of patience or simply the result of thinking that our idea is better than the ideas of others or that we are privy to some insights that others do not have.

I am constantly being told by a couple of brethren in my high priests quorum that obedience is the first law of heaven. (That is an interesting statement for which I would like to know the reference.) Then they quote the statement from the Book of Abraham which says: "And we will prove them herewith, to see if they will do all things whatsoever the Lord their God shall command them" (Abr. 3:25). I have always been uncomfortable with any approach to that passage in Abraham which puts emphasis on life as a testing ground (God has sent us to earth to test our faith to see if we will perform as well outside of his presence as we apparently did in his presence). I prefer to put the emphasis on the schooling experience (we were sent here to learn the difference between good and evil — why one works and the other doesn't).

The two principles (obeying blindly and researching on our own) are obviously not the same, but neither are they mutually exclusive. For example, in that passage in Abraham, we are told that God is interested in seeing if we will do everything that he commands us to do. One "commandment" God has given us is to exercise our own agency in constructive ways without his having to tell us what to do, because the power is *in us* to do much good (D&C 58:26–29). That seems to be one of the most fascinating paradoxes in scripture. God tells us to do what he tells us to do — and what he tells us to do is to do things without his having to tell us what to do.

So while it is common in Mormonism to consider life as a testing or proving ground, I think it is equally valid (and infinitely more beneficial) to think of it as a schooling place where we learn by having new experiences, by exploring ideas of our own, and thereby coming to recognize the consequences of such ideas and actions. Through this procedure we ultimately come to understand more fully the wisdom of God's laws and the reasons underlying those laws — and by understanding them to employ them more willingly with even greater faith. In fact, I prefer to think of it that way because by doing so I can embrace both of God's statements: the one in Abraham to obey and the one in the Doctrine and Covenants to work it out on my own.

As noted earlier the conflict between monism and pluralism has obvious analogues in the age-old friction between liberals and conservatives, and error lies at both extremes of the spectrum. Jesus often clashed with the Pharisees, the arch conservatives of Israel, but he also rejected the doctrine of the more liberal Sadducees, who readily embraced many aspects of Roman philosophy, moved freely in the company of the conquerors, and even accepted aspects of their lifestyle. Moreover, ancient Israel's problems in the Old Testament did not originate solely from too much exclusivity but rather from the very opposite — from foolishly embracing the novel ways and views of the peoples among whom they lived. Perhaps the Old Testament can be viewed as a case study warning against the dangers of unrestrained pluralism and the New Testament against excessive monism.

How much tolerance can we tolerate? I really have no resolutions to the problem nor even any brilliant guiding principles to suggest except perhaps to pass on one of B. H. Roberts's: "United in the essentials, tolerance in non-essentials"[6] — whatever that means. I suspect we would never get a total consensus on what falls neatly into either category. Judging from the ongoing, age-old battle between liberals and conservatives, I doubt that what I say will move those who have planted their minds in concrete at either end of the spectrum. What I have to offer, therefore, are simply my own feelings on the matter. These are some of the things I would like to see happen.

First, in the spirit of brotherly concern, I wish we could be a little less xenophobic and a little more ecumenical in our dialogue with other faiths. I realize that a study of other faiths can be disconcerting to the faith of any who have been taught that the church has a monopoly on truth. Nevertheless I believe there is a healthy way to enter into such a dialogue and to learn from those of other persuasions without diminishing faith in one's own religious views. In fact I have often seen young Latter-day Saints come away from such exposure with new, exciting insights into the strength of their own position.

We need to learn that in the economy of the world there is not a fixed amount of goodness and that recognition of the accomplishments of others need not somehow diminish our own. The story of Mormonism is a moving saga, and we have good reason to feel pride in it, but it is one among many. Many have also been deeply moved by the spiritual quests of some of the Catholic saints, of some of the Protestant divines, of Judaic rabbis, of Gautama or Mohammed and other founders of the world's great religions, and less-heralded men and women everywhere who have sought for and found meaning in the love of God and their fellow human beings.

This is not equivalent to saying that all roads lead to heaven — nor that authoritatively administered ordinances and covenants are not required nor that all churches are equally valid in the sight of God. But it does seem that God has prepared a standard of judgment which centers first and foremost in one's love of God and one's neighbors and that the powers and ordinances of the priesthood ideally flow out of that reservoir and not the reverse (as God tried so often to explain to wayward Israel).

Second, and perhaps this is simply an extension of what I have just mentioned, I would like us through comparison with others outside the faith to recognize our own deficiencies in areas where we are often lacking: in the arts, in scholarship, in humanitarian efforts which reach beyond the bounds of denominational concerns, to mention only a few. I wish we would get more involved as wards and stakes in activities to enrich our lives without expecting "the Brethren" or the Correlation Committee to do all of our thinking for us. I think there are many more important things we might ponder in our meetings than those we do now.

Third, I wish we could be a little more expansive in our study of what Mormonism means as revealed in our scripture and in our history. I wish we would be a little less authority ridden in our approach to scripture and not assume we have to await definitive statements from the General Authorities before we understand what scripture is all about or what it has to say. We would do well to review from time to time the statement made by Joseph Smith when Pelatiah Brown was brought to trial before a high council: "I did not like the old man being called up for erring in doctrine. It looks too much like the Methodist, and not like the Latter-day Saints. Methodists have creeds which a man must believe or be asked out of their church. I want the liberty of thinking and believing as I please. It feels so good not to be trammelled. It does not prove that a man is not a good man because he errs in doctrine."

Finally, I wish we would be less judgmental in our attitudes toward those in our wards and stakes who are different from us in terms of such things as middle-class lifestyles and modes of dress and those who see things in a slightly different light—especially in the realms of politics and economics. It is their church as well, and they also should have a chance for their own positive input.

I resist any in the church who teach that God is the Great Conservative (or Great Capitalist or Great Liberal) or that anyone on public welfare is out to live off the hard work of the rest of us. Economics is something the Lord is obviously very concerned about (at least where it touches on the problem of wealth and poverty), and I pain inside when I see my students taking the attitude that the poor are all of a common mold fashioned around a core of laziness. That is a good example of what I mean when I bring up the issue of conformity and its implication that everyone should be as I am.

My experience has suggested to me that most of us in the church in the United States know very little about poverty in general or even about the poor in the church. In the more articulate areas of the church, we are in the main a church of the middle class. Far too many of us are isolated from the poor. One of the most enlightening experiences I had in the church occurred while I was attending school in Syracuse, New York. Syracuse at that time was about the same size as Salt Lake City, but we only had one ward. That meant that Saints from all economic levels in the city came together in a common setting. Executives from Carrier and General Electric served as home teachers in the inner city areas where the bishop didn't even let the Relief Society teachers visit because of the high incidence of crime. (And many of those in the inner city wouldn't even come out to church because they were ashamed of their clothes and the way they were consequently treated by some of the members of the church. That was only one of their problems—bus fare was another.) Mormonism has become a middle-class or rich man's religion in our part of the world but not in others, and I wonder if the two will ever be able to understand each other.

When we moved back to Salt Lake, we lived for a couple of years in the Liberty Park area, which obviously is not inner city but comes closer. While living there I had occasion to speak at a few wards in the wealthier parts of the city, allowing me to contrast the difference in settings in which each segment worshipped. It was almost like two different churches socially. I wondered how some of my brothers and sisters in the Liberty Park area would be looked upon by the children of my brothers and sisters in the affluent Federal Heights area and vice versa. By virtue of the way we partition the wards geographically here in the West, we often keep the rich isolated from the poor and the poor from the rich. I'm not convinced it needs to be that way. Neither gets to see the problems nor strengths of the other.

My older children were reared in a very different church sociologically from my younger children. Because we later moved into an area of Salt Lake in which primarily older couples lived, my two older sons often had only one or two others in their priesthood quorums. Their friends who had moved from the neighborhood to the suburbs in Bountiful were going to Disney World in Florida for their major yearly ward outing. I have often wondered if there is not a better way to build economic understanding and the kind of unity of the faith I sense the Savior was advocating.

Even in our work with welfare recipients, we are isolated from them. When we go out to work for the poor, we go into the field or into the cannery with other middle-class members. Unless we become a bishop or a Relief Society president, seldom do we ever come face to face with the problems of hard-core poverty. But so many of our young people at the university seem to think they know all about it. Again surely there is a better way. There is a need for some good creative thinking about new ways to deal with such problems or at least of ways to develop empathy for those suffering.

Perhaps B. H. Roberts said it best in his now-famous article which touches on discipleship: "[Mormonism] calls for thoughtful disciples who will not be content with merely repeating some of the truths, but will develop its truths; and enlarge it by that development. . . . The disciples of 'Mormonism,' growing discontented with the necessarily primitive methods which have hitherto prevailed in sustaining the doctrine, will yet take profounder and broader views of the great doctrines committed to the Church; and, departing from mere repetition, will cast them in new formulas; cooperating in the works of the Spirit, until they help to give to the truths received a more forceful expression and carry it beyond the earlier and cruder states of its development."[8]

Roberts penned this in 1906, five months before William James delivered the Lowell Lectures. Obviously we have come a great distance since then. But we have even further to go in diminishing xenophobia and resisting appeals for a meaningless sense of homogeneity.

NOTES

1. William James, *Pragmatism and Four Essays from The Meaning of Truth* (New York: World Publishing Co., 1967), 90.

2. Joseph Fielding Smith, ed., *Teachings of the Prophet Joseph Smith* (Salt Lake City: Deseret Book, 1972), 303.

3. Ibid., 316.

4. Ibid.

5. Brigham Young et al., *Journal of Discourses*, 26 vols. (Liverpool: F. D. and S. W. Richards, 1854–86), 12:70.

6. *Sunstone*, Dec. 1979, 20.

7. B. H. Roberts, *A Comprehensive History of the Church of Jesus Christ of Latter-day Saints. Century I.*, 6 vols. (Provo, UT: Brigham Young University Press, 1965), 5:340.

8. B. H. Roberts, "Book of Mormon Translation," *Improvement Era* 9:712–13.

6.
Some Reflections on the Mormon Identity Crisis

Richard J. Cummings

How can organizations such as the Association for Mormon Letters, the B. H. Roberts Society, the Sunstone Foundation, and the Mormon History Association, organizations which are independent from the Mormon church, justify their existence? How can groups which have no official ties presume to serve as outlets for scholarly and creative writing on Mormon subjects and as constructive forums for significant Mormon issues?

I think that such associations are the direct outgrowth of a creeping identity crisis which is gnawing at the heart of Mormondom and that such groups provide partial but salutary resolutions of that crisis. Let me explain by relating a personal anecdote. As a graduate student at Stanford University, I belonged to a study group which was inquiring into the LDS concept of deity with all the zeal one might expect of a group of devout former missionaries. We needed to locate the King Follett discourse and thought we could find it in Joseph Smith's *History of the Church*, edited by B. H. Roberts. We did find the discourse listed in the table of contents of the first edition, but the pages listed in the table of contents were missing in our copy. They had been omitted at the time the volume was printed. Other copies of the volume had the same apparent defect. The page was numbered 301 on one side and 318 on the other.[1]

Frustrated and intrigued by this circumstance, we sent an inquiry to Elder Joseph Fielding Smith, who was then supposed to provide "Answers to Gospel Questions." We received a reply, which was as terse as it was prompt. The King Follett discourse was not published in the *History of the Church* because President Joseph F. Smith did not want it included. Of course this reply raised more questions than it put to rest, since no explanation was provided for President Smith's decision to delete the discourse.

I have since learned that B. H. Roberts, who believed the King Follett Discourse contained "many wondrous truths," was infuriated at the highhandedness of his publisher in deleting these pages. Roberts, who was a member of the First Council of Seventy, had been assigned to tour a mission just before the volume went to press and discovered the crucial omission quite by chance after his return. The only reason given for this action was a vague hint that "the Brethren" questioned the authenticity of the discourse. Roberts immediately had 10,000 copies of the discourse printed and distributed throughout the church at his own expense.[2] It is interesting to note that after all these years, B. H. Roberts's thirty-two-page pamphlet is still on sale at the Deseret Bookstores.[3]

This incident can serve as a paradigm of the phenomenon which concerns me. Roberts valued the truth as he perceived it, and he felt that the King Follett Discourse belonged in the *History* for two reasons. First, it was an integral part of church history. Second, it set forth theological truths which, however radical or controversial, were essential to a grasp of Joseph Smith's teachings concerning the nature of humanity and of God. President Joseph F. Smith, for reasons he never explained, decided that the historical and theological truths which Roberts prized so highly in the King Follett discourse could be overridden by considerations of personal or ecclesiastical expediency, and he suppressed the entire chapter. Although most of the doctrines contained in the discourse were already available to the public in the *Pearl of Great Price* and in the hymn "Oh, My Father," one can speculate that President Smith feared publishing it might prove embarrassing because it set forth the radical notion of a plurality of Gods and stressed literal anthropomorphism. The simple fact remains that the president of the church chose to exercise his prerogative as arbiter of all religious matters without apology or even the courtesy of an explanation.

However, it is also significant and reassuring that nothing indicates Roberts was taken to task for his rebellious gesture in publishing the pamphlet. He was fully vindicated posthumously in

1950 when the King Follett discourse was restored to its rightful place in the second edition of the *History of the Church*.[4]

What does all this have to do with an identity crisis? This incident provides a prototypical example of the clash between institutional authority and individual integrity and between the imperative of blind obedience and the claims of reasoned belief. Ultimately it exemplifies a fundamental conflict between a metaphysical pluralism emphasizing the eternal autonomy and the divine potential of humankind and a hyper-orthodox, theistic absolutism underlining the subservience of humanity to deity and the subordination of individual members of the church to the hierarchical superstructure.

It should be noted that although the tension between these conflicting views has greatly increased within recent years, it has always been present in the church. For instance, in support of the integrity of the individual, Joseph Smith stated categorically that "all men have the privilege of thinking for themselves upon all matters related to conscience. Consequently, then, we are not disposed . . . to deprive anyone of exercising that free independence of mind which heaven has bestowed upon the human family as one of its choicest gifts."[5] On the other hand, a few years later Apostle Heber C. Kimball admonished the membership of the church to "learn to do as you are told both old and young. . . . [I]f you are told by your leader to do a thing, do it. None of your business whether it is right or wrong."[6] He went on to justify this approach, re-echoing rationalizations for unthinking obedience offered over the centuries by totalitarian regimes: "If you do things according to counsel and they are wrong, the consequences will fall on the heads of those who counseled you, so don't be troubled."[7]

If over the years this conflict between enhancing and disparaging personal integrity has been seen at the highest levels of church leadership, then it stands to reason that it also will be found in the lower echelons. I know of no better example of this replication of the issue at the middle-management level than an unfortunate incident which occurred toward the end of my Uncle Benjamin F. Cummings's life.

Although Uncle Frank, as we called him, served many years as chair of the Department of Languages at Brigham Young University, his first love was teaching—particularly his courses on religion and ethics. As a natural outgrowth of that teaching experience and in response to requests from many of his former students, he spent his post-retirement years on a manuscript containing the fruit of his efforts over the years to synthesize his insights into "the origin and destiny of Man, the nature of God and Man, the creation, and meaning of existence."[8] His main concern centered around "the concept of the nature of the Self," and in developing this concept, he drew heavily on Joseph Smith's King Follett discourse.[9]

Since he was a member of the church in good standing and had enjoyed a distinguished career on the BYU faculty and since his manuscript provided affirmative and perceptive insights on the Latter-day Saint system of beliefs and values, he naively assumed that it would be publishable with some measure of official endorsement. He sent it through channels for consideration. After a year of the most tedious and disheartening bureaucratic runaround imaginable, he published the book at his own expense, entitling it *Eternal Individual Self*. Then came the crowning blow. He approached the man then serving as manager of Deseret Book—an individual he had always considered a friend—to ask if he could place a few copies there on consignment. After polite temporizing, this individual told him his request could not be granted. The only reason given for the negative decision in both instances was that "it might not meet with the approval of the Brethren." There is something heartrending about a benevolent old man, a kind of intellectual "true believer," having his life work rejected by the church which mattered to him more than all else. As Samuel Johnson wrote to Lord Chesterfield in response to the latter's belated offer of patronage, "I had done all that I could; and no man is well pleased to have his all neglected, be it ever so little."[10] Uncle Frank died, literally nursing his wounds, a short time after this final indignity.

With all due allowance for the unusually personal nature of this second anecdote, I would submit it can be seen as an updated lower-level recapitulation of the first anecdote. Both incidents led to the publication of an officially unapproved document bearing on the King Follett discourse, and although publishing the first was a gesture of defiance whereas publishing the second was an act of resigned desperation, both represent individual initiative and personal integrity in the face of hierarchical hostility or indifference.

The theological and ecclesiastical dichotomy producing this identity crisis can also be recognized in a fundamental split among members of the church. You can either lose yourself in the church, or you can find yourself in it. Many of those who lose themselves do so by renouncing their autonomous identity through blind obedience and mindless activism. Those who find themselves through Mormonism do so by taking literally the LDS maxim, "The Glory of God is Intelligence," and also the ideas in the King Follett discourse. We have an innate capacity which has been ours for all eternity and a God-given mandate in the gospel plan, urging us to think for ourselves and work out our individual salvation as we see fit.

Those who lose themselves in the church constitute the majority. Some of them minimize or even disregard the identity crisis because they find it convenient to refer their problems and worries to the "sure voice of authority" and let the Brethren think and plan for them. Those who seek to find themselves in the church have difficulty basing their convictions solely on faith-promoting experiences but must also wrestle with their misgivings, reach their own thoughtful conclusions however painful, and forge their individual testimonies in the crucible of private doubt and personal despair. As A. C. Lambert, former dean at BYU, aptly put it, those who seek to find themselves are "gnawed inside at times by . . . clear fallacies or even tyrannies in the strictly authoritarian pattern."[11]

One of the current trends in Mormonism which reinforces the tendency to lose oneself in the church can best be described as a kind of "cloning from the top." This trend probably follows from the rapid growth rate of the church, which produces a practical administrative need for increased conformity at all levels. A dramatic instance of this cloning trend was related by a close friend, who visited the office of one of the high-ranking apostles some years ago when Joseph Fielding Smith was president of the Council of Twelve Apostles. At one point in the conversation, the General Authority in question, wishing to dramatize the need for zealous obedience, pointed to a decorative picture hanging on one of the walls of his office. "If President Smith came into my office and expressed displeasure with that painting, the next time he came in it would have been replaced!" Contrast this ethic of total compliance even in areas of personal taste with the attitude of Brigham Young when he declared: "My independence is sacred to me—it is a portion of that same Deity that rules in the heavens.... The Lord has not established laws by which I am compelled to have my shoes made in a certain style. He has never given a law to determine whether I have a square-toed boot or a peaked-toed boot."[12]

So far I have given the Mormon identity crisis a predominantly anthropocentric focus. What I hope will be a fruitfully provocative question can shift the discussion to a more theocentric perspective: Do we worship the God of Truth or the God of Expediency? A scriptural basis for this question can be found in John 16:7 where Christ at the Last Supper declares: "Nevertheless, I tell you the *truth*; it is *expedient* for you that I go away; for if I go not away, the Comforter will not come unto you."[13] The Savior speaking of his divine calling uses "truth" and "expedient" in the same sentence and thereby suggests that at least for deity it is possible to reconcile the two. This reconciliation is further encouraged by the etymological fact that in 1611 when the King James version of the Bible was completed, the word "expedient" had only the positive meaning of being "clear of difficulties, fit and proper."[14] It was not until the eighteenth century that the term took on its pejorative and even Machiavellian meaning of being "conducive to advantage by going counter to that which is right."[15]

There is a tradition in the church that when literal truth and practical ecclesiastical advantage come into conflict, it is more godly to seek the advantage than to tell the truth. A classic example of this tradition occurred in 1850 when one of the leaders, though an ardent practicing polygamist with six wives, found it expedient under admittedly extenuating circumstances to deny the facts in these terms: "Inasmuch as this Church of Jesus Christ has been reproached with the crime of fornication and polygamy, we declare that we believe that one man should have one wife and one woman but one husband."[16]

A more recent example which demonstrates that the tradition of expediency is alive and well in the church today can be found in the strictures of President Ezra Taft Benson on what has been called the "New Mormon History." In an address delivered to religious educators in 1976, he said that "facts should not only be taught as facts; they should be taught to increase one's faith in the Gospel, to build testimony.... We would hope that if you feel you must write for the scholarly journals, you always defend the faith. Avoid expressions and terminology which offend the Brethren."[17] There is something disquieting about the manner in which that term, "the Brethren," can be invoked within the church as a vague sanction or threat. The phrase suggests a kinship not so much with the brotherhood of humanity as with the ubiquitous "Big Brother" of George Orwell's *1984*. It epitomizes the perverse arbitrariness of what Joseph Smith termed the "unrighteous dominion" exercised by "almost all men as soon as they get a little authority." Such authoritarian expediency negates the fundamental truths embodied in the King Follett discourse. Theologically there can be no conflict between what is true and what is expedient, but in the realm of practical affairs, whether ecclesiastical or secular, we must guard against a natural tendency to sacrifice truth to expediency.

Joseph Smith declared, it is "the first principle of truth and of the Gospel . . . to know for a certainty the character of God, and that we may converse with Him the same as one man converses with another, and that He was once a man like us."[19] If this statement is being supplanted by a definition of our nature as compliant pawns of an awesome God who is as inscrutable as he is inaccessible, then our identity crisis suggests that we are losing our unique theological moorings and are drifting into the mainstream of traditional Christian belief.

Hugh Nibley declared some years ago that "if Joseph Smith were to walk into a conference of the Mormon church today he would find himself completely at home; and if he were to address the congregation, they would never for a moment detect anything the least bit strange, unfamiliar or old-fashioned in his teaching."[20] However, anyone willing to face the Mormon identity crisis realistically must ask if Joseph Smith's imagined return to the church might not bear a closer resemblance to Christ's less-than-cordial reception in fifteenth-century Seville as conceived by Dostoevsky in the Grand Inquisitor episode of *The Brothers Karamazov* than to the cheery scenario depicted by Nibley. It should be clear by now that I am defending a value which I consider to be a distinguishing feature of Mormonism, which I personally hold very dear, and which makes me proud to be a defender of the faith: humans are the "eternal individual selves" and embryonic gods so stirringly described in the King Follett discourse as the core truth of the restored gospel. Of all the teachings of Joseph Smith, it is the one completely original concept which at the time he set it forth could not be found in any other philosophy, ideology, religion, or belief system on the face of the earth. In saying this I realize that I am contradicting Sterling McMurrin, who states that there is "nothing exclusive" to the "ideas that importantly characterize Mormon theology."[21] But for me this teaching offers at least one compelling piece of evidence that Joseph Smith was at the very least a uniquely gifted religious thinker.

There are two paradoxes relating to this core concept which ought to be noted here. First, those who lose themselves in the church, readily submit to "cloning from the top," and surrender their autonomy to the sure voice of authority, are also the ones who most readily consider themselves to be well along the way to godhood. But there is much irony in the notion that one can develop divine maturity and insight by abdicating initiative and trading integrity for spiritual dependency. It seems inconceivable that an unquestioning devotee cultivating tunnel vision on the way to perfection can somehow be metamorphosed into a god. Conversely, those who struggle to find themselves in the church rarely receive the coveted "seal of approval" so readily conferred on the unreflectingly obedient, and yet they achieve a breadth of feeling and a measure of understanding which is far more godlike than the mimicry of the mindless activist who would toady his or her way into the celestial kingdom.

The second paradox can be seen in the fact that the King Follett discourse has been given wider official distribution in the church during the last forty years than in the preceding ninety-four years since the discourse was first delivered, and yet the practical impact of the teachings it contains is less evident now than in the past.[22]

At the beginning of my remarks, I said that independent Mormon groups grow out of the identity crisis which is the subject of this essay. Clearly in the tradition of nineteenth-century blessing meetings and various twentieth-century study groups, such associations provide outlets for those heirs of the Mormon tradition who wish to think for themselves and express their own creative impulses and their deepest feelings about the restored gospel without feeling diminished or passed over by the official impersonal leveling process which is epitomized by "correlation."

As the church grows in size and strength there is less and less room for individuality. Church leaders often like to speak of Mormons as "a peculiar people," but woe unto individual members who choose to be "peculiar persons" in the way they view their church or practice their religion. I suppose this is simply in the order of things because, speaking in purely practical terms, if the church did encourage each member to give full expression to his or her every personal quirk and bias in doctrinal matters and religious practices, it could only lead to ecclesiastical chaos. On the other hand, those in positions of authority too often become obsessed with the fear that to tolerate even a modicum of spontaneous, individual input from the rank and file would be to open the floodgates to disaster. It would be encouraging if the leaders of the church could consistently grant to the membership the same kind of autonomy which my grandfather granted to my father as a boy of eight. Rather than impose his patriarchal will in the matter, the father simply asked the son very explicitly whether or not he wanted to be baptized and why. The fact that such autonomy is not the order of the day does create a practical and moral need for an appropriate setting in which to maintain one's integrity as an individual in a Mormon context. Thus groups like the Sunstone Foundation, the B. H. Roberts Society, the Mormon History Association, and the Association for Mormon Letters serve not only the best interests of individual members who wish to maintain, explore, and express their individuality, but they also serve the church's best interests. They too can help in the building of the kingdom.

NOTES

1. Joseph Smith, *History of the Church of Jesus Christ of Latter-day Saints, Period I*, ed. B. H. Roberts (Salt Lake City: Deseret Book, 1912), 6:301.

2. T. Edgar Lyon, "Church Historians I Have Known," *Dialogue: A Journal of Mormon Thought* 11 (Winter 1978): 4, 14–16.

3. Joseph Smith, *The King Follett Discourse: The Being and Kind of Being God Is; The Immortality of the Intelligence of Man*, ed. B. H. Roberts (Salt Lake City: Magazine Printing Co., 1963).

4. Joseph Smith, *History of the Church*, 2d. ed., ed. B. H. Roberts (Salt Lake City: Deseret Book, 1950), 6:302–317.

5. Joseph Fielding Smith, ed., *Teachings of the Prophet Joseph Smith* (Salt Lake City: Deseret Book Co., 1977), 49.

6. *Journal of Discourses* (Liverpool: Asa Calkin, 1859), 6:32.

7. William Clayton, *William Clayton's Journal* (Salt Lake City: Deseret News, 1921), 334.

8. Benjamin F. Cummings III, *The Eternal Individual Self* (Salt Lake City: Utah Printing Co., 1968), v.

9. Ibid., 33–34.

10. Letter cited in James Boswell, *The Life of Samuel Johnson* (New York: Modern Library), 154.

11. Asael C. Lambert, "Liberalism—Orthodoxy," notebook, Western Americana, Marriott Library, University of Utah.

12. John A. Widtsoe, ed., *Discourses of Brigham Young* (Salt Lake City: Deseret Book, 1977), 62–63.

13. Italics added.

14. *The Compact Edition of the Oxford English Dictionary*, 1971 ed., "Expedient."

15. Ibid.

16. *Three Nights Public Discussion between the Revds. C. W. Cleeve, James Robertson, and Philip Cater and Elder John Taylor of the Church of Jesus Christ of Latter-day Saints at Boulogne-sur-mer, France* (Liverpool: Published by John Taylor, 1850), 8.

17. Ezra Taft Benson, "The Gospel Teacher and His Message," Address in Assembly Hall, 17 September 1976, 7–8, Western Americana, Marriott Library.

18. *Teachings of the Prophet Joseph Smith*, 143.

19. As quoted by Stan Smith in "The King Follett Discourse: A Newly Amalgamated Text," *Brigham Young University Studies* 18 (Winter 1978): 201.

20. Hugh Nibley, *No, Ma'am, That's Not History* (Salt Lake City: Bookcraft, 1946), 46.

21. Sterling M. McMurrin, *The Theological Foundations of the Mormon Religion* (Salt Lake City: University of Utah Press, 1965), x.

22. For a summary of the publication history of the King Follett discourse, see Donald Q. Cannon, "The King Follett Discourse: Joseph Smith's Greatest Sermon in Historical Perspective," *Brigham Young University Studies* 18 (Winter 1978): 190–92.

7.
The Ghost of the Pioneer Woman

Linda Sillitoe

SHE IS SO ENGRAINED IN OUR CONSCIOUSNESS, PERHAPS EMBEDDED in our genes, that we fail to recognize her ghost almost everywhere — especially within ourselves. Yet *she* appears in generation after generation, changing her fashion to suit the times.

In Utah *she* is frequently Mormon. While she shares attributes with other pioneer women just as her descendants share with their contemporaries, she is also a particular within a universal.

We know her as she was. She crossed prairies, cooked biscuits over a campfire, bore children without anesthetic under a leaky cabin roof, and eventually was photographed (with every whalebone stay in place) posed on a rock pile, having dressed to the teeth to take lunch to her husband. Her faith did not falter when her children died of plague, her husband took other wives for godly reasons, or became a foreign missionary for several years. Then because he was engaged in his Father's business, she became a competent breadwinner. Within our living vision, she can still split rails or go east to medical school. She is midwife, healer, seamstress, and bakes wonderful bread.

As the women's movement belatedly reached Utah and Mormonism, we wanted to know *her* better; we, too, had frontiers to conquer, for American society was opening some hostile territory to women. We looked into the wilderness of possibility and found *her* bringing civilization to the sagebrush — our own expectations rose accordingly.

71

As a surge in women's history retrieved our heritage, our foremothers fired our imaginations and nourished our self-images. We watched Emma Smith wade the Missouri River with infants in her arms and clinging to her skirts. We cheered when she mobilized the Relief Society to fight her own husband's revealed order of plural marriage; we were as discreet about her defeat as we were when women's "auxiliaries" became "correlated" under the male priesthood. We watched Eliza Snow, Emmeline Wells, Susa Young Gates, and others exercise influence and creativity as Utah was born; and we saw women forbidden the exercise of spiritual gifts once the chaos of the frontier came under control. Our surprise was for their one-time power not their loss of power; yet at core we must have known both already through our mothers and grandmothers. For many of us, *she* is heredity and environment.

During the periods when there were no Indians, no Feds, no Germans, Italians, or Japanese for the men to fight, women's place became domestic again. Then the exertions women performed as pioneers and breadwinners found impressive if private expression in impossible standards of housekeeping, childbearing, or upon emotional battlegrounds. One bore children, the more the better; one did not divorce no matter what; one did not complain; one did not gossip; one did not admit failure. After all, *she* and her sister wives had raised a remarkable posterity.

Consider the story popular at one peak of this era when church president David O. McKay told Emma Riggs McKay that she had more important things to do than iron sheets. If one didn't iron sheets, one might prepare a casserole for the neighbors, or create silk flowers, or read the children a story, or prepare a Sunday school lesson, or quilt, or garden. This well-loved anecdote showed her meticulousness and commitment, his generosity and an apparent discontent with a woman who was more Martha than Mary. Martha, you see, prepares dinner, but Mary is more fun to take to lunch; for centuries we have tried to be both for men who have wanted both.

Another McKayism was that a woman should raise her voice inside the home only in case of fire. The guilt this adage helped to inflict is incalculable; the silence it perpetuated is lethal. Yet who could complain of such kindly dictates with campfire and outhouse only a generation or two in the past? *She* endured to the end with no modern appliances. If she wasn't happy, so much the greater her righteousness. Meaning that if our grandmothers, our mothers, if *we* weren't happy, we were probably doing what we were supposed to do; therefore we had our reward and could expect even more later.

She shadowed the superwoman rising in the national consciousness, gaining among Mormons a peculiar style. On the neighborhood level, jogging and early morning scripture reading were added to the list of home births, home pre-schools, home schools, and cottage industry. We filled our suburban split levels with home-ground wheat, canned peaches, gave lessons in everything from piano to smocking, sewed frilly dresses, and won extra points for tailoring husbands' suits. The invisible income we earned became a guiltless means of financial survival, though no less exhausting than entering the workforce. Still, *she* looked back at our weary, fervent faces in the mirror. In any gathering where a woman spoke, the rest of us spotted *her* in collars, stays, and cuffs behind the smiling face, impeccable testimony, and sweet voice of the Mother in Zion who did it all.

We saw *her*, too, in the pained eyes of the courageous women documented in "Mormon Women and Depression." We saw *her* again in "The Plan," a film in which Utah's Young Mother of the Year races from housecleaning, to home pre-school, to handball with her husband, tensely demonstrating how she won her title. But we rejected *her* in both shocking reflections, denying that *she* had anything to do with us. In our denial we were saying, "But we do it better—with laughter, with flexibility, with personal fulfillment," not realizing that we had just upped the ante.

In the late 1970s and early 1980s the real extremes erupted, as Mormon mothers urged or threw their children from balcony or bridge, gassed themselves and their children, burned down the house while the children slept. A few years later a younger woman who wanted out was slain with her baby because a Fundamentalist "revelation" had designated her "an alienated woman and her bastard child." Again we found these occurrences too exceptional to be relevant, failing to see *her* and ourselves behind the headlines.

Still, something spoke to us—for women's essays, poems, talks, and even testimonies relented. It became acceptable to express the hardships of pregnancy, birth, motherhood, widowhood. Even in these complaints we honored *her*, for they implicitly recognized her commitments. *She* was married; yet often among the journals and letters of women who had the time and education to record their lives, sister wives often lent *her* more independence than had the monogamous woman. Looking back, we tend to assign *her* both the status of marriage and the liberation of single life. It's a hard act to follow, especially when monogamous marriage is now the prime prerequisite for everyone. Choosing to be single, choosing not to have children, choosing an alternate lifestyle of any sort, remain peculiarly silent pockets within the national span of women's literature. Instead Eve, Sariah, and the pioneer woman herself became more accessible, more vulnerable, permitting an emotional leeway that produced more essays, more poems, more fiction. Yet *her* mountains, plagues, and trials of spirit could instantly reduce ours to molehills. How hard to admit that on one level, especially on Mother's Day, we hated *her* guts.

All of the above, of course, is a stereotype of *her* and of us. All of it, of course, is true. I, for instance, fancy sometimes that I created myself; I had no role model as a writer or journalist. With two radical decisions—which were linked, making them all the worse—I felt I tilted the universe and all its eternal implications. Against all *her* examples of faith and sacrifice, I chose to cease having babies rather than further compromise my health; despite *her* righteous priorities, I chose to spend my life writing even though I might not be any good. (This combination had the cheery potential of wasting my life and sealing my damnation.)

Nor had I any role model for my impatience with the icons, real and on paper, in blue suits or beards, on earth or in heaven, that teach my rising blood the meaning of "iconoclast." Yet *she* is all about me here and in another dimension; and when I reckon with myself, I reckon not with the dark suits no matter where they fit in the eternal chain of command. I reckon with *her*. Maria Ann, Elizabeth, Emma, Rosemarie, Fern, my mother, my sisters, my daughters. When I am discouraged or rebellious beyond reason or comfort, one of them comes. We didn't or can't or don't often talk about what matters; we all share the same informed current.

Long before I heard the phrase "Mother in Heaven," I knew my mother's mother was in heaven. Elizabeth became an "angel mother," dying when my mother, the last of eight children, was only five. Quite naturally my mother came as close as humanly possible to being an angel mother for the eight of us. As we grew up, she became a confidante, a friend, and the family diplomat, often at cost to her own feelings or health. Even as a very young child, I used to think about Elizabeth in heaven and mourn for my mother's loss. I was relieved when my mother did not die the year I was five. I later learned that my sisters silently shared the same fear, dreading each younger sibling's sixth year. Only much later did my mother, who created a storybook childhood for us, admit her resentment that she had been kept from her mother's sickbed. She learned of her loss early one morning when her two eldest sisters, Rosemarie and Ruth, burst into the bedroom, weeping. And then Elizabeth's own mother arrived at the house and told the traumatized children they had worked their mother to death. Ruth and then their father died several years later.

Elizabeth had done her share of pioneering in Nevada, American Fork, and later Murray. She was one of the first women in her community to drive a car, which she filled to capacity on Relief Society day. After her death, her grown daughters supported the family as the sons went on missions, to college, and then married. Rosemarie, a schoolteacher and musician, married late, at age forty, and moved to Downey, Idaho, becoming a pioneer of education and culture in the dusty farmland. Despite poor health, she worked extremely hard all her life and died at age fifty-seven. She was profoundly devout, orthodox, and obedient. Within her bookcase I discovered Art Linkletter and Ezra Taft Benson, then secretary of agriculture. Childless, Aunt Rosie fiercely loved all her nieces and nephews. At seventeen, I was asked to give her life-sketch at her funeral. But I cannot imagine sketching my life for her.

Nor to Emma, my father's mother, a self-effacing woman who in Poplar Grove raised six children and lost one to prematurity. I remember her warmth, her soft laughter, her confusion playing games at wedding showers, but mainly the creations of her hands— dolls in elaborate costumes, the embroidered, crocheted, and painted pillow cases and dresser scarves I still use. Even in death she didn't trouble anyone; just sat down in her easy chair, gave a little cough, and was gone. When I look at the plaque in my office that reads, "Nobody Knows the Trouble I've Been," I doubt she would understand.

Still, there is Maria Ann, a great-grandmother, who at age ten stood at the top of Emigration Canyon, spied the settlement below, and ran all the way down the mountain. She didn't know what she was racing toward; she would support a family after her husband deserted her, turn down his requests to take him back, and then dictate a letter shortly before her death asking to be resealed to him in eternity.

Such ambivalence is inherited. If some strait-laced ghost forever chides, "You are not what I expected," Maria Ann is still poised somewhere in my mind at the top of the canyon, willing to dash into whatever the future holds.

Recently I've thought often of Fern, a middle child in my mother's family; a tomboy, Fern would outdare her brothers standing on the tracks beside the house as a train bore down on her. In the 1950s, Fern became one of the few female managers in the church bureaucracy, one of the few women whose death was ever mentioned in general conference. She had a full-time career, she traveled, she entertained, she nurtured. When I think of Fern, I think of abundance—dozens of chocolate cookies, blond brownies, wedding dresses for friends' daughters, Thanksgiving dinners, Fourth of July parties for the whole tribe. Yet Fern had married disasterously, a secret she protected while lavishing her attention on her siblings' children, becoming in the absence of grandparents the hub of the family wheel. Divorce was not an option; even after seven years of leukemia, she didn't see death as an option. She would not jump from *any* track until the last moment, and died incrementally, horribly at age forty-two, leaving her secret at last exposed.

It took years for our family to accept and deal with Fern's death. My sister Susan and I were adolescents then. Years later we found ourselves confronting leukemia again, this time in Susan's third daughter. Abby fought the disease for years, but by the time she was five she could not be kept in remission. The day the fateful tests came, Susan talked with Abby about death and about heaven, naming loved ones who were already there. When she came to Fern, Abby suddenly leaned over and kissed her mother's cheek. "What was that for?" Susan asked.

"I had a dream, and Aunt Fern was in the dream. She told me to give you a kiss for her."

My mother stoically related this incident that evening at a family meeting called to prepare for Abby's bone marrow transplant that now would not occur. As a family, we coped better than we had with Fern's dying. We fasted, we prayed, we hoped and grieved, but we faced Abby's death. Hurting, we let her go.

Fern shadowed our lives again when we learned that another sister, Janean, was in an abusive marriage. Even a generation later, divorce was still not an option; she was protecting her secret. In long conversations we explored her feelings and philosophy, and finally the myth Fern had died upholding helped to free Janean. When she left her husband, she felt she had to hide herself and their babies for a time. We met at an inexpensive apartment we had located quickly through a friend. Janean looked around the shabby rooms, out the windows at the alley and broken bottles, and back at me. Hesitantly she signed the lease. As she climbed into her car, she smiled radiantly, joyously as if she were not about to plunge into the unknown. At that angle in the sunlight, for the first time I saw her resemblance to Fern—an aunt she hadn't known but now regarded as a kindred spirit.

Recently as I lay exhausted and waiting for sleep the night before one daughter left home to launch a new life, I felt Fern nearby. She had stayed on the tracks, I realized sleepily—but when we jump, she is with us.

Several years ago when our children were in grade school we read them a newly-compiled history filled with the drama of my mother's stalwart family, plagued by ill health and early death. Repeatedly, commitment, determination, drive, and faith were emphasized as the hallmark virtues until our perceptive and all-too-objective children began to remark upon the costs. Within the family tradition, only serious illness could deter one from duty, if even then; suddenly my radical choices seemed downright healthy.

Within the history are letters between Fern in Salt Lake City and Rosemarie in Downey, in which each lists her projects—Fern's baking, the status of her gardens, the bridesmaids' dresses she is sewing, her office work, and Rosemarie's accounts of the children she has tutored, the chorus she accompanied, the lessons she has given, the stream of overnight guests. For years Susan and I have sent our lists back and forth across the continent, all we, our husbands, our children, have done, all we have yet to do. We beg our mother, who turned in midlife from a bread-baking homemaker to a business partner, not to work so hard. Between family birthday parties, church work, and frequent rescue missions, she denies she's overdoing it, then admonishes us. It does little good. *She* listens in on our telephone conversations, *she* edits our letters. Nor are we uniquely afflicted. Over lunch our women friends exchange lists, accomplished and pending. From the next table *she* eavesdrops, knowing we can do the impossible.

Yet as we come to know *her* and ourselves, perhaps we can learn to acknowledge not only her accomplishments but her heartaches. We can project her sympathy rather than her judgment. We can believe, if we try, that *she* remembers how the campfire leaped to scorch the biscuits, the maddening leak in the cabin roof, the singe of jealousy, the noise of loneliness. We can assume *she* preferred her complexities to ours. We can picture the ghost of the pioneer woman or a mother in heaven approaching with outflung arms. We can tell our daughters they are doing fine.

Though I like to think that becoming a writer defeated the myth, it's hard to maintain the delusion. When stressed, I start baking (not for myself, of course, but for whomever I can think of to feed). I want Fern's brownies and cookies at family parties for those of us who remember and for the little cousins who delight in swiping them just as I did. In the midst of writing *Salamander: The Story of the Mormon Forgery Murders*, Allen Roberts, my co-author, was sometimes nonplussed to arrive ready to work on the manuscript and find me up to my elbows in flour.

Once I moved my office home for the last round-the-clock months of writing, we fed the occasional cop and our researchers became part of daily life. Kathy Ballard (another sister) and Lin Ostler watched me synchronize folding the laundry to feeding the printer and agreed no man could ever accomplish what we would. The official editorial "retreat" (involving all men but me) was held at our home—meaning day-long critiques of the rough draft, plus accommodating a houseguest, and hosting an evening party for all involved with the project. That night in the kitchen, Lin gave me her most feminist look and said, "You shouldn't be doing this; you're writing the book." I shrugged. Try telling that to *her*.

Sometimes I think I see changes; then I am not so sure. No one has mistaken me for an angel mother. Neither of my daughters is an expert cook or seamstress, though, like my son, they forage well. However both have high expectations for their lifework and for rich relationships. If *she* watches over their shoulders, I hope she is more encouraging than formidable; she probably looks a lot like their grandmothers and I worry that she looks like me. Imprinted at a formative age, my youngest began writing a novel at eleven and is now plugging away at six of them. Recently she counseled another junior high student, who tends to be an over-achiever. Warned my daughter, "As long as you never write the first novel, you'll be okay."

8.
The Phenomenon
of the Closet Doubter

D. Jeff Burton

MORMONS PRIDE THEMSELVES ON BEING A TIGHT-KNIT GROUP. BUT there are groups within the group—investigators, believers, non-believers, jack-Mormons, the faithful, temple recommend holders, cultural Mormons, inside-outsiders, the active, and the inactive. I would like to add another group to the list—closet doubters. Other names might include faithful doubters, faithful disbelievers, active disbelievers, or hopeful doubters.

During my mission to Japan, I chanced upon a super-active but genuine non-believer—my first encounter with a faithful doubter. She was serving in the Young Women's Mutual leadership and was extremely active in the branch. I had been talking to her about bringing her non-member friends and, in the course of conversation, tore open her soul, learning the secret of her disbelief.

I thought at the time that an active non-believer must be a rare bird. But it was a little like learning a new word. What you think is a rarity is suddenly recognized all around you. Since that day in 1962, I have had the opportunity to cautiously identify and speak confidentially with a number of people who have invisible memberships in the group I am calling closet doubters.

What is a closet doubter? A closet doubter, as I have chosen to define it, is an active Latter-day Saint who has secretly rejected (or disbelieves) one or more of the fundamental tenets upon which today's church is based such as Joseph Smith's First Vision, the divine calling of Joseph Smith as prophet, the Book of Mormon as an

angel-delivered history of the early Americans, and the divine origins of Joseph Smith's later revelations as published today in the
Doctrine and Covenants and the Pearl of Great Price. But closet
doubters continue to be active in the church. They attend meetings,
teach Primary and Sunday school, hold temple recommends, serve
in quorum presidencies and bishoprics, and some work for the
church. Outwardly they are little different than other active members. Notice that I do not include persons who have lost both belief
and activity or those who have announced their loss of belief.

Most doubters I have met were in their mid-twenties to mid-
forties. Younger men and women apparently have neither the experience nor the education necessary to catalyze the complex reactions
necessary to become a closet doubter. Older persons, if they were
doubters in their younger days, seem either to have slid into in-
activity, have regained their beliefs, or have come out of the closet.
Doubters tend to be educated and well read, particularly in history,
psychology, philosophy, or science. Most have studied the scriptures
and appear well versed in church history. They come from strong
church backgrounds. They are often the offspring of traditional
Mormon families, or they have been committed converts. Many are
returned missionaries, many have married in the temple, and most
have close and important ties to the church such as daily jobs or
church callings.

What do they believe, how did they become doubters, and
why do they stay active? Personal belief seems to be a continuum and
is in constant flux. The extremes are represented by "I know (something) is true" and "I know (something) is not true." The typical
active church member professes a positive belief in the Joseph Smith
story. Closet doubters by definition must (secretly) admit to disbelief
or profess negative belief. But, and this is a most interesting condition, most closet doubters appear to have had a relatively strong
belief before becoming doubters. Though doubting the authenticity
of the official Joseph Smith story, most express commitments to the
goals, principles, and practices of today's church. The reasons are
often summarized as follows: The basic principles of the church
came from the Bible and thus are not the invention of Joseph Smith.
Principles of life, caring, sharing, kindness, honesty, integrity, and
sacrifice are universal, true, noble, believable, and worthy of support. Programs associated with obtaining a good education, main-

taining health, and providing public service are worth supporting. Most say something like, "The church may not be true in the 'one and only true church' sense of the word, but there's certainly nothing better out there." Few are expecting to find any "true church," and few are searching for separate avenues to satisfaction. In fact settled doubters appear to be relatively happy, fulfilled people with little hint of hate or vindictiveness.

This is surprising given the anguish most experience during their "de-conversion." Before finally admitting to a lack of belief, they experience an agonizing transition period, usually measured in years and often filled with insecurity, alienation, anger, and confusion. This in-transition state is accompanied by feelings of guilt ("I mustn't feel this way" or "I shouldn't have read anti-church literature"), feelings of denial ("Of course I believe" or "It's just a stage" or "I've got to stop thinking this way" or "I'm being tried, so it'll pass if I just stick it out"), feelings of shame ("What kind of a sinner must I be?"), feelings of anger ("Why me?"), and feelings of loneliness ("I'm the only one with these thoughts and problems" or "There is no one who understands"). Given these emotional conflicts, it is not hard to understand why some seek professional counseling.

After finally facing up to the fact of their disbelief, most say they feel an odd sense of relief and a freedom not felt during the transition. They say things like, "The truth has made me free" and "Free agency finally means something." Some feel good in making a free choice to participate without the guilt that hovered over them during the transition. Some express an "understanding" of their circumstances and are able to rationalize, even to cherish, this "understanding." This is not to say that confirmed closet doubters are free from inner conflict. Far from it. It just takes another form and is usually more tolerable.

No doubter's motives for continued activity are as pure and idealistic as I have just described. Most doubters are tied to the church like birds are to the earth. It might be okay to fly a bit, but gravity eventually has its say. These gravitational ties include being married to a believing spouse (you don't further weaken the relationship), the desire to give children strong and stable support (to keep them away from drugs, sex, and anti-Christian behavior), family traditions and history ("It would hurt my mother if I went inactive"), job security (particularly if you work for BYU or the church), a social life revolving around friends who are believers (how do you attend your friend's or more seriously your son's temple wedding if you're inactive?), and of course fear (the official Joseph Smith story might be true after all).

Some justify their continued activity as contributing to improvements in church practices they consider wrong, weak, or embarrassing. Those often mentioned include the black issue (now resolved), the temple ceremony (now altered), women's rights (now the object of considerable activism), the stress on unquestioning obedience, the missionary system, the self-serving nature of church programs, poor teaching methods, questionable business practices, authoritarian leadership, and the lack of vertical dialogue from members to leaders. Many express feelings of hope—hope that perhaps in the great scheme of things God indeed does recognize the church, hope that perhaps doubters can find happiness, hope that they can do some good through the programs of the church, and hope that by some small chance they might be wrong about their doubts.

Where are these doubters? How many are there? And why do we hear so little of them? I believe they're everywhere in well-established church locales, but they're probably more concentrated in the larger cities, on university campuses (including BYU), and in the more affluent wards.

What predisposes one to become a faithful doubter? How does one lose beliefs of a lifetime? These are the most difficult questions and cannot be answered definitively in this essay. But education does seem to be one factor. Faith-shattering personal experiences (for example, death of a loved one or a family member becomes a disbeliever) may trigger the syndrome. Other factors include inquisitiveness, difficulties with authoritarian leadership or male-oriented leadership. Knowledge of church history seems to be common. Access to the arguments against Joseph Smith and the Book of Mormon is often present. It is, however, difficult to tell which comes first, the doubts which lead to search for the confirmation or the detracting literature which leads to a loss of belief. I have noticed that for many people it is a stepped process: a little doubt supported with a little justification leading to more doubt, the search for more justification, and so on.

What impact do doubters have on the church? They are definitely involved in events at the local level, and because of their educations and skills, they often have positions of leadership and influence.

Now I would like to introduce a few closet doubters. This will make the phenomenon more personal, more real.

From a late-thirties housewife, mother of three, graduate of BYU: "By the time I finally recognized my lack of belief, my children were in school. My children don't need any disruptions in their lives at this time. It's hard enough. My husband is in the seventies quorum in our ward. What alternatives do I have? If I start talking now, it could hurt his work. I'm not unhappy. I just find it easier to keep quiet about the whole thing. My husband is very good about it all. I don't think he really understands. He thinks I'm going through a stage, a trial. It's easier for me to let him think that. Anyway maybe I am. I hope he's right."

From a forty-year-old high priest: "The big thing left for me now is hope. I hope, I pray that things will turn out right. I hope the church is true, but I really doubt it. It's worth staying with. Faith and hope. It's all I have, all I need, truly."

From a mid-thirties salesman: "My contact with the world started my journey into doubt. I went through a terrible period of guilt and hate. I was impossible to live with. I lost my first wife over this, so I find it easier now to keep quiet. It's not my place to be going around destroying people's faith. The Lord showed me the light. Let him show others if that is what the Lord wants for them. Who's to say what the big picture is? I'm the last to say that I have all the answers."

From a member of a bishopric: "I have really thought seriously of quitting it all. But every time I do, all the positives seem to outweigh the negatives. I can influence things somewhat in my ward, but I have to be really careful not to do anything to embarrass the bishop. I try to stress the positive aspects of the gospel — sharing, love, giving. You know, those things that people need really bad. I always keep the Word of Wisdom, pay my tithing, and, you know, that kind of stuff. But I do it because of my position and for my wife and kids. My kids don't know a thing, but my wife knows everything. In a way she's coming to see things from my point of view — you know, starting to support me in subtle ways."

From a twenty-two-year-old woman, a convert of six years, studying in Utah: "I joined because of my friends. The only friends I have now are in the church. If I start causing trouble, I'll lose my friends. I know it sounds childish. But my parents were very upset when I joined. I don't have close ties at home anymore. I hope to marry a Mormon. And nobody wants an inactive Mormon."

From a twenty-three-year-old woman, just married to a non-Mormon, and a Ph.D. candidate: "Father-in-Heaven has answered my prayer — the church teaches Christian principles, but it isn't perfect. But before I received those answers, it was rough. I didn't know who to turn to or who might help. I hope to get my husband to join. I feel a lot of peace with myself, knowing that I love the church for its people and for what it can do for people, not for what it is, was, or purports to be."

From a twenty-two-year-old returned missionary, presently studying history at the University of Utah: "I never did gain that burning testimony everybody kept talking about. In fact my faith in Joseph Smith disappeared during my mission. It's just too incredible! My mom and dad spent a lot of money . . . most of their savings to send me to England. If they knew . . . well, it would hurt them. I think I'll be pretty active. I'm not searching for a quick fix from anybody. The church is my life and my guide. I'm just going to be cool and use what's good for me."

These closet doubters keep their interpretations hidden within. Sometimes even spouses do not know the extent of their doubts. Why is this? First, there is the fear of being ostracized or worse put on the pedestal reserved for investigators. Mainstream believers often remain aloof and feel uncomfortable around those who ask too many questions or demonstrate a doubting nature. More seriously, believing members often interpret a rejection of their beliefs to be a rejection of themselves. The second reason for secrecy is the fear that the chance for meaningful church participation might be reduced. More than a few worry that a non-sympathetic bishop might deny them a temple recommend — although some have confided in bishops who have been understanding and supportive. Third, the church has said on several occasions that it can tolerate divergent beliefs as long as those beliefs are held personally and no attempt is made to sway others. This is interpreted to mean, "Remain a silent doubter." Finally, many express the thought that it is not their place to destroy or alter the faith of anyone else. Coming out of the closet might be a shock for those whose testimonies rely on the strength of another's faith.

Doubters learn to speak truthfully but discreetly. When asked to bear testimony, it comes out something like, "I know that the church teaches correct principles; I know that the Lord answers prayers; he loves every person; we must all work out our own salvation." Can they accept the church president as prophet, seer, and revelator? Some say, "Why not? Certainly no one else is. I can accept the possibility that he is a prophet." Others say, "I accept with what faith I have." The question about the prophet is probably the hardest one for those seeking a temple recommend to answer. Even if they can deal with that question, getting a recommend is often difficult because it vividly reminds the doubter that he or she is living a life which is not totally candid.

This need to maintain secrecy, to sometimes practice a subtle dishonesty, isolates the doubter and creates internal conflicts. Such conflicts are the successors to those experienced during the often hellish time of transition.

Will closet doubters survive? The outlook is hopeful. Most individuals I have met appeared relatively stable and happy. Some have gone inactive. Some have gone inactive and then returned again, still doubting but hoping. Many have come out of the closet. One I know has developed a strong belief again.

As for the future, several scenarios have been suggested to me. The first, somewhat farfetched, proposes that in time some of them will quietly reach positions of substantial authority in the church and initiate changes in the claims made for Joseph Smith. Another scenario has their numbers and influence growing over the next few generations until the LDS church reaches the present status of the Catholic church: many not truly believing the official story but staying and supporting because of inertia, culture, tradition, and family ties. A third scenario pictures the church somehow inviting and accepting disbelievers into open, full, and active fellowship.

During recent years the church has conducted systematic investigations of belief, faith, and activity among active members. The results have not been made available to the general public, but I have been told that studies suggest 5-10 percent of active Mormons may be quiet faithful skeptics. What the church is doing about this, I don't know.

I believe skeptical thinking is expanding, particularly among younger members of the church. The reality of increasing skepticism cannot be overlooked forever. We will have to face up to it, and the sooner the better. As William James put it, "He who acknowledges the imperfectness of his instrument, and makes allowance for it, is in a much better position for gaining (and sustaining) truth than if he claimed his instrument to be infallible" (*Varieties of Religious Experience* [1902]).

Even though the number of doubters may be increasing (and perhaps *because* of the increase), I believe it is easier now than in past years for a faithful skeptic to be accepted among unruffled believers. I also think it is easier to come out of the closet. And I believe it is useful to do so, and encourage secret doubters to prepare themselves and their families for that step.

I also see benefits in being faithful—particularly to oneself and to God, but also to the church. Traditional blessings are available to members who remain faithful to the teachings of Christ and who continue to participate in the church. Additionally, inactive troubled people can have little effect on the things that trouble them. If you want to change things, you have to participate. The church has shown a willingness to change things in response to reasoned and supportive criticism.

But again, religion and church activity are personal choices and everyone must eventually choose the path which makes the most sense.

9.
Woman as Healer
in the Modern Church

Betina Lindsey

"I WENT TO MY BISHOP TO DISCUSS SOME THINGS THAT HAD happened in my life, and I asked him for a blessing," the woman began cautiously.

"There were circumstances in my family—my husband was inactive, and I had an unusual position in our home. The bishop said I should call upon the power of the Melchizedek Priesthood to bless my family and those whom I loved and served. Not too long after, my son, who has serious attacks of croup, woke up one morning coughing. Within about five minutes, he couldn't breathe. I ran into the bathroom [carrying] him, turning on the shower to create steam, but he was turning blue and couldn't get any air. Someone called the ambulance. Meanwhile my son was sitting on the toilet seat and I sat in front of him on the bathtub edge. Suddenly in a natural, instantaneous response, I laid my hands on his head and said, 'As E_____'s mother, I call on the power of the Melchizedek Priesthood' and I blessed him. I had always prayed desperately for him during these attacks, but this was the first time I had ever laid my hands on his head and invoked the priesthood. While I was speaking, his head slipped forward from under my hands and fell on my lap. He was asleep! His breathing was even and relaxed. By the time we arrived at the hospital, they questioned why we'd brought him at all. I'd given blessings before—with women, to other women—for infertility, alcoholism, and depression; but I'd never quoted priesthood authority until that morning with my son."[1]

I consider this woman to be a pioneer; but rather than exploring new terrain, she is rediscovering the vast landscape that was once the freehold of Mormon women—the domain of woman as healer—and from which for three generations women have been exiled.

Evidence from Mormon women's journals, diaries, and meeting minutes tell us that from the 1840s until as recently as the 1930s, LDS women served their families, each other, and the broader community, expanding their own spiritual gifts in the process. Even now the ward fast and the temple prayer circle symbolize the union of our spiritual community; for by uniting together to seek healing for others, we heal ourselves and our community. But because the church now defines blessing the sick as a function of male priesthood authority, we all suffer from the loss of women's potential as healers.

In the last decade or so, a growing number of LDS women are questioning this externally imposed limitation. They not only desire to exercise such a gift but discreetly practice it. I personally believe that those who feel the desire either to bless or to be blessed should claim their right as members of the "household of faith" to lay hold of that gift.

This essay argues four points: (1) There is clear historical and scriptural precedent for women as healers. (2) The process and gift of healing are ungendered. (3) The Mormon health blessing contains ritual elements which resemble elements in the healing rituals of other cultures. (4) The LDS church could benefit collectively by officially recognizing the resource that women healers represent. I conclude by urging a broadening of women's service.

Since the founding of Mormonism, women have constituted an important spiritual and community resource through exercising the gifts of healing. Linda King Newell's well-researched "Gifts of the Spirit: Women's Share" traces the LDS tradition of women's spiritual gifts, particularly speaking in tongues and healing the sick. Indeed our nineteenth-century foremothers give their sisters an unparalleled heritage of spiritual activism. It is a sacred tradition with which we should all become more familiar.

It begins in Nauvoo when the women of the Relief Society frequently pronounced healing blessings upon each other. Elizabeth Ann Whitney remembered receiving her authority to so act by ordination: "I was . . . ordained and set apart under the hand of Joseph Smith the Prophet to administer to the sick and comfort the sorrowful. Several other sisters were also ordained and set apart to administer in these holy ordinances."

The April 1893 *Young Woman's Journal* describes the healing gifts of Lucy Bigelow Young, a plural wife of Brigham Young and a St. George temple worker: "How many times the sick and suffering have come upon beds to that temple, and at once Sister Young would be called to take the afflicted one under immediate charge, as all knew the mighty power she had gained through long years of fastings and prayers in the exercise of her special gift. When her hands are upon the head of another in blessing, the words of inspiration and personal prophecy that flow from her lips are like a stream of living fire. One sister who had not walked for twelve years was brought, and under the cheering faith of Sister Young she went through the day's ordinance and was perfectly healed of her affliction."[2]

Nor did these women consider themselves to be radical innovators. Instead they harkened back to the scriptures to find the exercise of such gifts promised in abundant measure — and, what is more, promised upon condition of faith irrespective of gender.

The promise of healing power came directly from Jesus Christ to anyone born of the Spirit: "And these signs shall follow them that believe; In my name they shall cast out devils; they shall speak with new tongues. They shall lay hands on the sick, and they shall recover" (Mark 16:17–18). The Book of Mormon prophet Moroni corroborates that "all these gifts come by the spirit of Christ; and they come unto every man [or woman] severally, according as he [or she] will" (Moro. 10:17).

Bruce R. McConkie, a Mormon official, wrote in *Mormon Doctrine*, commenting upon gifts of the spirit: "Faithful persons are expected to seek the gifts of the Spirit with all their hearts. They are to 'covet earnestly the best gifts' (1 Cor. 12:31; D&C 46:8), to 'desire spiritual gifts' (1 Cor. 14:1), 'to ask of God, who giveth liberally' (D&C 46:7; Matt. 7:7–8). To some will be given one gift; to others another."[3] "And again, to some it is given to have faith to be healed; and to others it is given to have faith to heal" (D&C 46:19–20). Women are clearly included within this injunction to "seek the gifts of the Spirit with all their hearts."

Although the contemporary church does not theologically exclude women from healing—because all believers in Christ have access to the same gifts—they are excluded from performing the ordinance. They cannot anoint with olive oil, seal the anointing, and pronounce a healing prayer calling upon the power of the priesthood. This exclusion, as Newell carefully documents, is not a theological sanction but rather a matter of evolving church policy.[4] Because the church has since the 1960s defined and correlated itself as a "church of priesthood" in what I believe is an effort to make men take their responsibilities more seriously, it has systematically excluded women from many gray areas, equating "adult male" and "Melchizedek Priesthood."

Healing by the laying on of hands brings together three sources of power: (1) God's power, transmitted through the conduit of human action; (2) faith, exercised both by the recipient and by those participating in the blessing; and (3) the healing power of the healer, a gift which is apparently an act of free grace from God to certain individuals who in their turn are free to exercise or withhold it.

There is no indication in Mormon theology that priesthood is in itself the healing power; rather it is an avenue for exercising that power. Quite obviously in earlier days of the church Melchizedek priesthood was only one avenue. Women's faith was still another. It is difficult to estimate how many priesthood holders possess the gift of healing. But it seems that any worthy priesthood holder can serve as a conduit for God's power. It also seems likely that even when the priesthood holder is not worthy, a blessing pronounced upon a faithful member of the church may still be heard and answered due to the faith of the recipient or a loved one.

Restricting healing blessings to Melchizedek priesthood holders only is a limitation on women's spirituality. One husband observed, "If one of the kids has a sore throat, I don't think it's time for a blessing. If they were in the hospital with a serious illness, then it would be different." His wife, however, felt differently: "I think a blessing can be a preventative to worse things to come. He says I worry too much. I feel helpless sometimes; and because he's the one with the priesthood, I'm put in the position of nagging him into giving a blessing he doesn't feel is necessary."

Another woman expressed dismay at the "routine" nature of priesthood blessings. When a woman in her ward became seriously ill, the first sister's husband administered to her but "for the next weeks, I and the other Relief Society sisters went into her home and nursed and took care of her and her children." When she recovered this sister mentioned the event to her husband who gave her "a blank look because he didn't even remember the sister's name or administering to her." She concluded, "I think it was the prayers and nursing by the sisters in the ward that healed her."

To my knowledge there has never been a suggestion that women's faith is not efficacious individually or collectively in healing or that a woman's supplication for healing herself or another is inappropriate. Thus contemporary Mormon women are not officially forbidden to heal. Rather they are forbidden to engage in the rituals of healing.[5]

An interesting example of the church's uneasiness with women's exercise of the gifts of healing was an instance reported by David Miles Oman during a question-and-answer session at a Mormon Women's Forum lecture on 8 June 1989. During his mission in France in 1972, he and his companion taught the gospel to a woman who "had the gift of healing": "The gift first manifested when she was a child, and she had laid her hands on a pet and it was healed. We gave her all the literature about the church, and she read everything and joined, becoming a faithful member. The mission president visited her in regard to her gift of healing; and though he recognized her ability to heal as a spiritual gift from God rather than [from] Satan, he requested she not use or demonstrate the gift for now." We can speculate on the mission president's motives: a desire not to confuse members by having two sources of healing authority, a concern about the inevitable questions of appropriateness that would arise, even a desire to help the woman fit more swiftly into the conventional roles assigned an LDS woman. I wish I knew whether this woman accepted the limitation imposed upon her and whether she is still an active member of the church.

Another woman I interviewed had been promised "the gift of healing in your hands" in her patriarchal blessing. She said, "I use the gift mainly for my own children and family, drawing out the pain with my hands. Afterwards I sometimes feel drained. I haven't used the gift outside the family, though I find when I visit the sick I can

talk with them, and my voice, in some part, soothes and helps them."
I think with longing of the blessing this woman could be to her ward.

Church leaders emphasize "spirituality" and "worthiness"
in calling upon gifts of the spirit. But for Mormon women that
emphasis becomes a double bind when the symbol and avenue for
spiritual manifestations within the church is male priesthood. In
essence Mormon women become spiritually dependent on male
priesthood holders for healing ordinances even though Mormon
theology gives them equal access to God's power. It is particularly
ironic in light of recent statements by church leaders about the
spiritual "superiority" of women that the hierarchy allows no official
avenue for women to exercise this gift.

Virtually every society has created a ritual for attuning an
individual with divine source as a channel of healing or other important spiritual gifts for the community. Ritual use of language and
symbols is central in such empowerment rituals because symbols
both represent and objectify power.[6] Within Mormonism sacredness
attaches to both the consecrated healing olive oil and to the ritual
language. They communicate power, awaken faith, and enhance the
individual's sense of personal empowerment. The priesthood
holder speaking words which have been spoken many times in similar settings puts himself in touch with the power that has operated in
previous settings. I believe that priesthood mediates power from a
divine source to the human setting by distinguishing key structural
symbols and moving them into a proper relationship to allow power
to flow through them. In other words an ordinance creates order.
The priesthood power to establish order through ritual lies at the
root of the healing process.[7]

This priesthood ordering or alignment was historically extended through the use of physical objects when the healer was
distant from the source. We see a scriptural example of such "porta-
ble charisma" in Moses' brazen serpent, which had the power to heal
any Israelite bitten during the plague of serpents (Num. 21:8–9). A
modern example occurred in July 1839 in Nauvoo and Montrose
during a malaria epidemic. Joseph Smith, who had been healing the
sick, was waiting to return to Nauvoo when a father asked him to
heal his three-month-old twins: "Joseph told the man he could not
go, but he would send some one to heal them. He told Elder
Woodruff to go with the man and heal his children. At the same time

he took from his pocket a silk bandanna handkerchief, and gave it to Brother Woodruff, telling him to wipe the faces of the children with it, and they should be healed; and remarked at the same time: 'As long as you keep that handkerchief it shall remain a league between you and me.' "[8] In his book *Early Mormonism and the Magic World View*, D. Michael Quinn cites additional examples of healing handkerchiefs, including those of Lorenzo Snow, Newel Knight, and Caroline Butler, as well as a cape that Joseph Smith consecrated for healing purposes.[9]

Consecrated oil, which is usually blessed for its healing function in quorum meetings as a semi-private act of a united brotherhood, is the only ritual object currently involved in healing. Women, by being excluded from priesthood meetings, are not witnesses to the consecration.

Some faithful Mormon men regularly carry consecrated olive oil with them in tiny pocket-size vials. Women may be responsible for seeing that the family medicine chest contains a current supply of consecrated oil. But because they were barred from using oil at the same time they lost the privilege of giving blessings, they are also distanced from the close proximity that some men retain to this holy object. Consecrated oil is part of the washing and anointing portion of the temple ritual for women as for men. But the increasing strictness surrounding anything temple-related has made the use of oil for women even less accessible rather than more comfortable and familiar.

The second part of the healing ritual is the laying on of hands and the pronouncing of the prayer of administration in which, even though the wording is not specified, certain elements must appear as cited in the official priesthood handbook. Laying on hands is an important part of the ritual. To the best of my knowledge, all Mormon prayers outside of the temple are pronounced with arms folded and hands clasped except for four: confirmations, ordinations to the priesthood, settings apart, and blessings of healing. As non-priesthood holders woman participate in none of these, so even the ritual posture—a circle of men with their hands on the head of the recipient—is associated with male priesthood functioning.

Many of the women I've talked to express hesitancy about laying hands on someone's head because they are afraid that assuming this "priesthood posture" will be seen as inappropriate. Some of them avoid the problem by establishing physical contact in other ways during the pronouncing of a blessing: hands on shoulders, holding hands, and so on.[10]

A precious twentieth-century document for Mormon women is a written form of the blessing to be pronounced in a washing, anointing, and sealing before childbirth. It was recorded in the minutes of the Oakley (Idaho) Second Ward Relief Society between 1901 and 1910. This excerpt combines the use of consecrated oil, ritual language, and the laying on of hands:

"We anoint your back, your spinal column that you might be strong and healthy no disease fasten upon it no accident beleff [befall] you, Your kidneys that they might be active and healthy and perform their proper function, your bladder that it might be strong and protected from accident, your Hips that your system might relax and give way for the birth of your child, your sides that your liver, your lungs, and spleen that they might be strong and perform their proper functions, . . . your breasts that your milk may come freely and you need not be afflicted with sore nipples as many are, your heart that it might be comforted."[11]

The blessing continues in what could be a revelatory tradition for women in modern times. Nineteenth-century blessings — and obviously this one as well — involved the anointing and blessing of the area of the body mentioned in the blessing, a depth of ritual that now exists only in the temple. The question of propriety is no doubt one reason why male leaders of the church accepted the administration of women to each other and why laying hands on only the head of the recipient accompanied the narrowing of pronouncing blessings to males.

The portion of the women's prayer quoted above does not specify the authority of the women. Some contemporary women who give blessings circumvent the problem by developing another category of blessings: the "mother's blessing." One woman, a single parent to whom the idea of women holding priesthood seemed "spooky," admitted giving her son a mother's blessing. A guest speaker at a Young Woman's values night in my ward said, "My husband travels a lot on business; and sometimes when he's gone, if a child is sick, I give a mother's blessing." She quickly added, "It isn't like a priesthood blessing."

Alternatively some temple-endowed women have blessed others by invoking "the authority with which we were endowed in the temple" or "by the power of our united faith in the Lord Jesus Christ." Still others invoke the priesthood of their husbands. A friend of mine who is a gifted healer reports, "I've given my husband a blessing, and I lay my hands upon him and cite his priesthood authority, which I share." The mother who blessed her croupy son invoked the Melchizedek priesthood without specifying who held it.

Imagine with me a scenario in which LDS women could serve each other with the spiritual rituals of healing blessings—important in physical health—and blessings of comfort and counsel—important in mental health. An immediate result would be to strengthen the church at large by increasing the spiritual autonomy of more than half its members. One single woman expressed her frustration at the "inaccessibility" of blessings due to the inaccessibility of priesthood holders. She describes her ward's demographics as "180 families which are mostly single women" and "about twenty priesthood holders." She has had no home teachers during the five years she has lived in the ward. The "home teaching" is done by visiting teachers by special permission. "And if you're sick, it better be on Wednesday night because you can only catch the bishop on Wednesday."

A second immediate result would be an increase of faith because women would be released from the very real and very crippling fear that they are "doing something wrong" and may be punished by the community. It breaks my heart to hear of beautiful experiences like the two that follow where even as the women experience the unquestioned outpouring of the Holy Ghost, they still draw back fearfully.

One woman told me about a time when she was twelve and her father was dying from Lou Gehrig's disease. Early one morning her mother called her awake—her father had quit breathing. She ran downstairs to be with him while her mother called the bishop and the family. "Somehow I felt I could do something about it. I held his hand in mine and sincerely prayed as best a twelve-year-old could do. After a moment, his eyes opened. He looked at me and asked, 'What did you do? My lungs lifted and I could breath again.' He said he'd been fighting to live all night and felt like he should give up. It was a very humbling thing, and we both knew that the Spirit had worked through me. A few months later, he did die; but we were all better prepared for it by then. I hadn't labelled it as a healing blessing until years later when I was listening to a lecture about experiences like this in the church. I've always felt a need to heal hurts of others. I would like to have the option to use that power, but I'm not sure what makes it okay to call on it. It seems the natural thing to do. I would like to have that permission."

In the second example a Relief Society president, concerned about some sisters with serious physical and emotional problems, asked if they would like some of the sisters to come and pray with them. "They all thankfully agreed. I called sisters in the ward who were close to them—friends and visiting teachers—and arranged for baby-sitting for a half hour or so. The sisters made every effort to be there. Some left work. We knelt in a circle, and I said the prayer. It was a deeply spiritual experience for everyone involved, and I would have liked to have put my hands on their heads as I prayed; but I felt we were on the edge as it was, with no priesthood [holder] present."

It is ironic, given the tradition of Mormon women's healing, that the new tradition makes women apprehensive about using their spiritual gifts. How can we encourage Mormon women to cross the borders of timidity and comfortably use these gifts in the service of others? Although the ordination of women to the priesthood would remove objections to women performing the ordinance of administration and overcome the hesitancy Mormon women feel about practicing healing, ordination is not an event they can control or bring about. Rather than wait for women's ordination, I think it is wiser to concentrate on what women themselves *can* do. I would hope that women who feel drawn to healing would "earnestly seek" this gift and prayerfully exercise it, appropriately uniting with those who have the complementary gift of faith to be healed and strengthened by those who have the gift of faith in the Savior.

I hope that women will break the silence of the last three generations regarding the exercise of this gift and share their experiences with each other and with selected men in appropriate ways. We need to tell each other stories, not only the stories of our foremothers and their healing experiences but also our own.

Some may feel that if such sharing becomes "public," it will be seen as a "publicity stunt." I have talked with literally dozens of

women about this topic. Although many—not all—feel disap-
pointed at their exclusion from the church's official healing rituals
and some who are aware of the history resent the injustice, none are
angry at the church or inclined to use a healing occasion to try to
embarrass the church or put public pressure on it. In fact I would
suspect that anyone prompted by such a motivation probably would
not be a successful healer.

Book of Mormon prophet Moroni promises: "All these gifts
of which I have spoken, which are spiritual, never will be done away,
even as long as the world shall stand, only according to the unbelief
of the children of men. . . . Wherefore, there must be faith; and if
there must be faith there must also be hope; and if there must be
hope, there must be charity" (10:19).

Unbelief is not the reason Mormon women no longer practice the gift of healing. Rather there exists much faith but no legitimate avenue to exercise it. Even though the Relief Society motto is
"Charity Never Faileth," the church's distancing of its women from
blessing circles has diminished Moroni's vision of faith, hope, and
charity to plates of chocolate chip cookies and tuna casseroles. Mormon women are trained for private charity, Mormon men for public
priesthood power. Those in one realm are required to close their
eyes to the other realm. The disconnection of charity from power,
unfortunately, ensures that charity is powerless and licenses power
to be without charity.

The instructions in Doctrine and Covenants 46:7–9, which
preface the list of gifts given to the members of the church, contain
important cautions. One of these cautions is against sign-seeking,
self-aggrandizement, or other unworthy personal motivations. But
the other important caution is against being deceived "by evil spirits,
or doctrines or devils, or the commandments of men." I agree that
these cautions against self-deception and temptation are important;
I wonder if the warning against "the commandments of men" may
also be a caution against our own traditions that may unnecessarily
limit and restrict us.

The rest of Section 46 of the Doctrine and Covenants is a
celebration, a promise, and an encouragement to exercise spiritual
gifts: "But ye are commanded in all things to ask of God, who giveth
liberally; and that which the Spirit testifies unto you even so I would
that ye should do in all holiness of heart, walking uprightly before

me, considering the end of your salvation, doing all things with prayer and thanksgiving. . . . And that ye may not be deceived, seek ye earnestly the best gifts, always remembering for what they are given; For verily I say unto you, they are given for the benefit of those who love me and keep all my commandments; and [her] that seeketh so to do; that all may be benefit that seek or that ask of me."

NOTES

1. I personally collected all of the accounts used here from the individuals who were directly involved. However, because healing blessings are officially assigned to men who hold the Melchizedek priesthood and because many Mormon men feel uneasy about autonomous action by women, many Latter-day Saint women feel vulnerable in speaking openly of giving and receiving blessings from women. To preserve their anonymity and to respect their privacy, I use no names in any of the contemporary accounts of healing blessings by women which I quote.

2. Linda King Newell, "Gifts of the Spirit: Women's Share," in *Sisters in Spirit: Mormon Women in Historical and Cultural Perspective,* eds. Maureen Ursenbach Beecher and Lavina Fielding Anderson (Urbana: University of Illinois Press, 1987), 115, 124.

3. Bruce R. McConkie, *Mormon Doctrine* (Salt Lake City: Bookcraft, 1966), 314.

4. Newell, 111–50.

5. The exclusion does not specifically forbid women's participation. Rather women are silently excluded by the instructions of who may participate and how. The current policy on blessings of healing and blessings of comfort and counsel appears in the *General Handbook of Instructions* (Salt Lake City: Church of Jesus Christ of Latter-day Saints, March 1989), 5–4 and 5–5: "Normally, two Melchizedek Priesthood holders administer to the sick. . . . If no one is available to help, a Melchizedek Priesthood holder has full authority to both anoint and seal the anointing. . . . Fathers may give their children blessings on special occasions, such as when the children go on missions, enter military service, or leave home to go to school. A family may record a father's blessing for family records, but it is not preserved in Church records."

6. Meredith B. McGuire, *Ritual Healing in Suburban America* (New Brunswick: Rutgers University Press, 1988), 227.

7. Ibid., 213–39.

8. Joseph Smith, *History of the Church of Jesus Christ of Latter-day Saints, Period I,* ed. B. H. Roberts (Salt Lake City: Deseret Book, 1912), 4:4–5.

9. D. Michael Quinn, *Early Mormonism and the Magic World View* (Salt Lake City: Signature Books, 1987), 222.

10. The practice of laying on of hands is not uniquely or distinctively Mormon. The practice is known worldwide and across time. Its sources are unquestionably the intuitive and instinctive gestures of comfort that we offer a hurt child: laying a palm on a feverish forehead, kissing a scrape to make it well, patting a weeping child. The formal laying on of hands is the oldest form of ritual healing, known to virtually every religion. Rock carvings in Egypt and Chaldea (Iraq) and cave paintings in the Pyrenees that are 15,000 years old depict individuals in a formal attitude of laying both hands on another person. The Roman emperor Vespasian (A.D. 70–79) had the reputation of healing blindness, lameness, and mental illness with a power in the palms of his hands. The Spanish conquistadores found Native American shamans and brujas of both genders laying on hands (Diane Stein, *The Book of Women's Healing* [St. Paul, MN: Llewellyn Publications, 1988], 116–17). North American Pentacostal congregations practice the ritual widely today.

11. Newell, 130–31.

10.
At Home at Sea: Confessions of a Cultural Mormon

Scott Kenney

I GREW UP BELIEVING THAT IF I EVER LOST MY TESTIMONY, THE world would come to an end. That was foolish, of course, because a testimony is simply a truth about my beliefs and judgments about life. I can only "lose my testimony" when I lose consciousness. But what I meant then was that if I no longer believed that God lives, that Jesus is the Christ, that Joseph Smith was a prophet, and Ezra Taft Benson is a living prophet today—if I no longer believed *those* things—I would fall into apostasy, and there is an incredibly power-ful aura of "evil" surrounding apostasy. Apostasy is a black hole. If you fall into apostasy, everything will come crashing down and your whole life will be in ruins. Apostates lie, cheat, and steal; apostates fornicate, adulterate, and do drugs.

The recommended preventative for apostasy is faith. Alma says that we should plant our seeds in faith. Then if the seed is good, it will grow and our faith will be increased. I would add, stay with that tree as long as it produces fruit and you find the fruit nourish-ing. But if despite your best efforts the tree withers or its fruit sours, you might try doubt. Until you doubt that the old tree will ever produce again or that it is the only true and living tree upon the face of the whole earth, you probably won't try a different solution.

Have faith to doubt. Liberals gesture at doubt. They "question." But few dare to really doubt. Jesus said, "Seek, and ye

shall find; knock, and it shall be opened unto you." In search of truth
I came up against doubt. I knocked on the door. It opened. I walked
in and found nothing. Nothing. Just me. No bogeyman to drag me
down to hell, no slippery slope to crime and debauchery, just me. I
continued to the next door. I knocked. It opened. I walked in. Nothing there either. Just me. And so on, door after door, opening windows and portals, letting the sun shine in and fresh breezes blow.
Doubt produces nothing, and that is a valuable contribution. It
cleans out the clutter. Then you can get down to the real business of
life: creating.

For me real theology is necessarily autobiographical. At this
point, therefore, I should tell you something about my background
and personal experience. I was born Mormon, fourth or fifth generation on both sides. My father was a returned missionary as was his
father; both of my mother's parents had served on general boards;
and growing up in Utah, my friends and acquaintances were also
Mormon. I learned why things are the way they are and what behaviors are acceptable from my family and culture. And I gained the
approval of parents and peers by conforming to those standards.

Early morning seminary was the first setting where I was
conscious of being not only accepted but also valued as a member of
society. Our teacher was Richard Marshall, and the course was the
Book of Mormon. Brother Marshall's enthusiasm was infectious, and
he instilled in me a passionate interest in the Book of Mormon.
Reading it cover to cover was a rite of passage initiating me into the
adult world, and obtaining a testimony of its divinity certified my
maturity. I thought that if I could master the scriptures I would not
only keep a commandment, but I would learn how to win blessings
from God that would enable me to achieve in all aspects of my life. In
the next four years I read the Book of Mormon five more times, the
Old and New Testaments twice, the Doctrine and Covenants twice,
the *Articles of Faith, Jesus the Christ*, and other popular church books.
At eighteen I was so anxious to be a missionary that I could think of
little else, and arrangements were made for me to work the summer
for Truman Madsen in the New England Mission.

By the time I was old enough to be officially called as a
missionary, Boyd K. Packer had replaced Truman as president. The
difference in style could not have been greater—Madsen's was a
world of evangelical fervor and spiritual gifts, Packer's of unques-

tioned commitment to priesthood authority. Madsen was the exemplar of my years as an enthusiast, Packer my first model of a true believer.

President Packer's favorite themes were the responsibilities and prerogatives of the priesthood, his favorite metaphors militaristic. The priesthood was the army of God. God communicated his orders to the troops through the priesthood chain of command. We foot soldiers had only one responsibility — to follow our file leaders. As long as we followed this order of priesthood, the gates of hell could not prevail against us.

After a year in the mission office, I was given an opportunity to demonstrate my understanding of this doctrine. My companion and I were driving President Packer and Henry D. Taylor to Logan International Airport. "Brother Kenney," Elder Packer asked, "what would you do if your mission president asked you to do something that you did not understand — like jump in a lake?"

"I would do it. I would jump in the lake."

"But what if it wasn't just something you weren't sure about but was something you thought was wrong?"

I knew the answer, but for the first time sensed it might be a lie. "I would do it anyway."

"Even if you thought it was wrong?"

"Yes, because the mission president has responsibility for the entire mission, and the Lord will hold him accountable. My duty, my stewardship, is to follow my priesthood leader."

That experience was the beginning of my transition from Latter-day Saint to liberal Mormon. Somewhere near the surface of my consciousness, I knew that neither the priesthood nor the church could come between me and God, between me and my personal accountability.

At the University of Utah's Institute of Religion, Reed Durham presided over my early years as a liberal. Through the late 1960s and early 1970s, Reed introduced his students to controversial issues in church history, always with ample documentation and plausible interpretations — and he always allowed his students to draw their own conclusions. I like that. I had learned behavioral management from President Packer. I learned historical perspective from Brother Durham. Doctrines did not fall from heaven fully formed but emerged in social context and were adapted by human hands to fit the circumstances. God necessarily spoke in terms that could be understood by human beings with finite conceptual abilities. Even prophets process revelation through human organs, the result not always being divine. With my new understanding, God's fingerprints were less clearly visible, but the opportunities for human participation were magnified. It was an exciting prospect for me. I decided to obtain a degree in theology and become an institute teacher. I was accepted at the Graduate Theological Union (GTU), a consortium of nine Catholic and Protestant seminaries that functioned as Berkeley's graduate school of religion.

During my years at GTU, I was constantly struck by the meticulous care and sensitivity of biblical scholars, by the richness of their interpretation. Biblical theology was milk and honey to my taste. Church manuals, which had never been particularly palatable, became even harder to swallow, and favorite Book of Mormon passages were eclipsed by deeper themes, more eloquently expressed in the Bible. In American historical theology, I discovered thinkers spanning three centuries who captured my imagination as no Mormon writer ever had. I felt shame for the paucity of the Mormon intellectual tradition. We who claim the glory of God is intelligence seem to value it so lightly.

Though I was actively involved in the student ward, my best friend was a Roman Catholic priest, Al Ede. Ten or fifteen years my senior, Al had grown up in Dubuque and had immersed himself in the theology of Thomas Aquinas. Then came the Second Vatican Council, and like so many conservative Catholics, Al's life was transformed. He understood full well the struggles I was going through. Like me Al had come to GTU to obtain a doctorate in American historical theology. He also served in a multi-ethnic parish in Fremont, and one week he invited me down to meet his people. It was the first non-Mormon service I had ever attended. Naturally I took all my Mormon judgments about the sterility of formal liturgy. What a surprise! Al delivered a powerful sermon, members addressed one another with love and affection, and wonderfully contemporary religious songs were beautifully performed in a folk song idiom, all building to a sacred and joyful celebration of the eucharist. From beginning to end it was one of the most moving experiences of my life.

I stood with Al at the door as his parishioners left the service. I will never forget the look in their eyes as they greeted and embraced him. Those people—Philipino, Portuguese, Mexican, Italian, and Caucasian—were truly blessed to be served by this man of God, and so was I. Our lives were uplifted and enriched by his words, his caring, his presence. Four years later, administering the eucharist in Dubuque, Al suddenly collapsed. An aneurysm in his brain. He died almost instantly, and a light went out in my life. But through my association with a Catholic priest named Al, I learned that God is found not in thunderbolts, dogmas, and commandments but in love and service, commitment and joy.

Our principal teacher and mentor was John Dillenberger, who had just stepped down after ten years as president of GTU. Dillenberger had been a student of Paul Tillich—and a teacher of Truman Madsen. After graduating from Union Theological Seminary and Columbia, Dillenberger had taught at Union, Princeton, Columbia, Harvard, and Drew and then brought together nine Catholic and Protestant seminaries to form the Graduate Theological Union. He had made his academic reputation as a Luther expert, and his anthologies of Luther and Calvin writings are standard textbooks.

For three years I took nearly every class he taught. He assigned only primary sources—church fathers, scholastics, reformers, puritans, revivalists, transcendentalists, liberals, social gospelers, neo-orthodox, moderns, and post-moderns. Four to seven hundred pages a week. I was stunned. Week after week I was exposed to theologians who had addressed core issues in vastly different contexts but all with a breadth of vision and command of the tradition unknown in my Mormon experience. Dillenberger began each class with historical and biographical background and then initiated discussion. He approached each reading fresh, open to new possibilities from his students. His own analyses were brilliant, never presented as the final word but as openings to new direction.

One day near the end of my first quarter, we left class together. He headed for his office and I for another class in the same direction. He wanted to know how I was getting along. We chatted for a few minutes, and then he changed the subject. He reminisced about *his* student days. When Tillich went on speaking tours, he let Dillenberger use his campus office. As he talked, he pulled a ring of keys from his pocket and began twisting off one silver key. He would be gone for a week or ten days now, Dillenberger said, handing me the key. My apartment was some distance from school, and I was welcome to use his office. No dove descended, and there was no voice from heaven, but I wouldn't have noticed. I had come on a pilgrimage to the temple of knowledge and the gatekeeper not only welcomed me in, he handed me the key. Of course, this was only *my* experience. When I reminded him of the incident years later, Dillenberger had forgotten it completely.

Nevertheless we visited and lunched together often, and Peggy Fletcher, Al Ede, and I were always included when the Dillenbergers invited students to their quarterly dinner at their home in the Berkeley hills. I will always be grateful to Jane Dillenberger for opening doors to the visual arts that enrich my life, but in retrospect their greatest gift was community and the opportunity to discover that rather than dividing people into camps, real religion brings people together, real religion transcends differences and flourishes in diversity.

It was the early 1970s, and Vietnam, Watergate, and nuclear weapons were on all of our minds. To my Catholic and Protestant colleagues, church was *the* center of social activism. They were not only *permitted* to express themselves on social issues in church, they were *expected* to speak out and to take action as a Christian *obligation*. They demonstrated against the war, lobbied against sexism, and sponsored food and clothing drives. My Mormon friends, on the other hand, generally shunned social issues. In Sunday school we praised the steadfastness of our pioneer ancestors. In priesthood we sat through yet another lesson about being member missionaries, while in Relief Society single sisters were reminded of the importance of motherhood.

If there was a God and if he loved us, I had argued on my mission, why would he not call a prophet to guide us in these troubled times as well as anciently? Now that question came back to haunt me. Where *was* the prophetic spirit for our times? Was it with the Saints, who took out an endowment once a month for someone who had died three or four centuries ago, or with the sinners, demonstrating in the streets against the napalming of *living* men, women, and children?

Who were the real prophets for the modern world? Once Mormon prophets believed "it is not given that one man should possess that which is above another, wherefore the world lieth in sin." Once Mormon prophets believed that marriage and sexual relations between consenting adults were no one else's business. Once Mormon prophets championed the rights of minorities and decried the tyranny of the majority. What had happened to those prophetic oracles? Who were the prophets of sweat shops and child labor laws? Who were the prophets of Selma and Montgomery? Who were the prophets of nuclear disarmament, ecology, and human rights? Had God really copped out on global issues, or was he speaking through non-Mormon channels?

If Mormonism was really going to contribute to the kingdom of God on earth, I concluded, leadership would have to come from the people; it was not going to come from their managers. If members could only see themselves as leading characters rather than as spear carriers in the divine drama, there would be no limit to what might be accomplished. My concept of religion was transformed from a system of revealed doctrine and ordinances to personal values, social renewal, and aesthetic awareness.

For ten years I was an active participant in what I hoped would become a Mormon Renaissance. During those years the issues I had put on the back burner—issues I had been unable to resolve in an orthodox context—gradually moved forward, first pushing orthodox configurations out of position and then eliminating some and elevating others. The following four examples illustrate the nature and scope of these changes.

First, my understanding of scripture and revelation was transformed by biblical studies. Though I had read it several times, much of the Old Testament had remained a sealed book, portraying God and prophets in ways that were incomprehensible to me: God tests Abraham with an order to murder his son; the ingestion of rabbit is forbidden because though they chew a cud, rabbits do not have split hooves; Elisha calls two she-bears out of the woods to devour teasing children; Isaiah wanders around Jerusalem stark naked for three years. What kind of religion is this? A historical religion, I learned, presented in a historical document. Historical documents inevitably reflect points of view no longer shared by the modern reader. And one of the pleasures of history is unraveling long-forgotten assumptions of ancient texts.

The Book of Mormon, on the other hand, contains little if anything that does not have a nineteenth-century ring. Equally significant, there are few early nineteenth-century issues not treated in the book. Both are to me sufficient and compelling arguments for its nineteenth-century origin. The book didn't need gold plates to be prophetic because it addressed the spiritual needs of the people in a way that gave them hope and purpose. It took a stand on controversial issues while maintaining a sense of continuity with tradition. Would that a Mormon could produce a work of comparable value for twentieth-century Saints.

Second, Jesus. The Jesus of my Mormon upbringing had never been a compelling figure. Because God was the father of his body, Jesus could postpone his own death as long as he wanted. He had direct access to angels and could talk with God whenever he wanted. He could perform any miracle he wanted whenever he wanted. He never sinned or did anything wrong. Because he was perfect, only Jesus could satisfy a thing called "the demands of justice." Enduring excruciating pain, bleeding from every pore and finally giving himself up to crucifixion, Jesus "paid" for everything I would do that was wrong. I would be resurrected and, if I kept his commandments, would not have to suffer for my sins (although trying to keep all those commandments seemed a *lot* like suffering for my sins).

I liked the parables and beatitudes of Jesus and his emphasis on love and forgiveness, but it was difficult to model my life after a god who became an itinerant miracle worker, who never sinned, and whose crowning achievement was crucifixion and resurrection. Atonement I had to take on faith, though really it was more an intellectual assent, for it never seemed "real" to me.

(A brief digression: It has always seemed strange to me that "eternal principles" like the "demands of justice" are never around when you need them. They have a way of popping back into the pre-existence or leaping forward into eternity when it comes to the nitty-gritty of human life. They seem "operative" only as theological constructs.)

On the other hand the Jesus described by biblical scholarship came alive as a powerful manifestation of God's relationship to humankind. Paul and the authors of Mark and John knew no-thing of the virgin birth. For them Jesus was fully human, struggling with temptation, identifying with sinners, speaking of God not as lawgiver or commander but as a loving Father, who pardons sinners and welcomes the unwashed. In raising Jesus from the dead, God disclosed the true nature of his participation in the human condi-tion. In Jesus, God invites all to celebrate the reconciliation of human and divine.

Third, the plan of salvation. According to Mormon theology, God first lost a third of his progeny to Satan; then he set up mortality as probation for the remaining two-thirds. The catch was that no one would remember their pre-existence, and hardly any would be told the standards by which we would be judged. The vast majority would pass through this life without the foggiest idea of what it was all about. Their main purpose would be to "obtain a body," of which they would soon be deprived for several thousands or millions of years and which would someday be given back to them, only it wouldn't be the same body, it would be a resurrected body, so the experience of having a body, if they remembered it at all after all those eons of time, would really be quite different.

I can see why martyrdom-seeking Christians and fourteenth-century serfs experienced life as a test, but it has never appealed to me. Surely God, the father of my spirit, had a pretty good idea of what I was like before I came here, and if I couldn't accept God's judgment in the pre-existence, how will mortality improve my atti-tude? Don't all those babies born in disease-ridden cultures have an unfair opportunity to die before hormones and the philosophies of the world overpower them?

This "plan of salvation" minimizes mortality for nearly ev-eryone but Mormons and predisposes God's "elect" to arrogance. For me life is too sacred to be trivialized in this fashion. I am still constructing my own "plan," and at this stage it is admittedly vague. But the principal components are Mormon in character: "joy" or its near-equivalent is the purpose of life, and Alma's "restoration" principle—we get what we create—the governing axiom; men and women are free agents with an equal opportunity to create meaning and value for themselves despite the inequity of circumstances.

Finally, the Mormon emphasis on commandment-keeping showed me the inadequacy of ethical behavior alone as means to a rich and rewarding life. There are so many "oughts" and "shoulds" that there is precious little time or energy for the "joy" that all this commandment-keeping is supposed to produce. "Faithful," "obedient," "long-suffering," "hard-working," "supportive" are the watchwords, the attributes of Latter-day Saints on the road to perfection. In contrast, "spontaneous," "imaginative," "creative," "passionate," "innovative," and "playful" are secular, inferior—attributes of those who have lost the way. I have concluded that if I do live forever, I would rather spend eternity with the Mozarts and Tina Turners of the terrestrial kingdom than all the Brother Browns of the celestial.

In retrospect these observations seem so simple that it is sometimes difficult to understand why I did not see them sooner. The answer is that it served me not to see them. As a child I had seized the iron rod and followed it along the straight and narrow path. Back and forth, back and forth, forth and back. As long as I believed in Joseph and the plates, in priesthood and commandments, in pre-existence and the plan of salvation—as long as I believed in these things my life had meaning and structure, and I was approved by my family and culture.

But the straight and narrow path was also rather short, I found, and led to a dreary plain. As I developed a stronger sense of self, when I no longer relied on the church for personal identity, I began to see in the distance an oasis. I determined to take a little trip to see what I could see, and packing my Book of Mormon and Doctrine and Covenants in my knapsack, set out for the oasis, with the full intention of returning to my home with exotic treasures to benefit my people.

The oasis proved to be everything I had dreamed of and more. It was filled with all manner of fruit to nourish the soul and please the senses. There were gorgeous panoramas, soft summer breezes, and crystal clear nights. I drank long and deep from liberal waters, and it was good. As I became more aware of alternatives and gained confidence in my abilities to sort it all out, I realized I had left orthodoxy behind for good. But until I no longer *needed* the Book of Mormon to be the word of God, until I no longer *needed* someone else to get God's answers for me, I could not let go and so could not create anything else.

Others grow in orthodox ways. They find their lives exciting, productive, and fulfilled in an orthodox context. I respect their experience. I only speak of my own.

Eventually liberalism heightened my capacities and stimulated me to seek promised lands beyond the seas. John Dillenberger once described faith as being at home at sea. There is no straight and narrow path on the open sea, no iron rod — and there are no guided tours. I have made a few voyages on open seas since becoming a cultural Mormon, each time returning with the feeling that I had come closer to the source of it all. The source, I know, is not "out there"; it is "in here," and I seem to come closer the farther I go. Each time I leave, it is with greater appreciation for the iron rod that brought me to a vision of the oasis and with gratitude for my friends there.

To be sure, seafaring faith does not come without a price. In addition to the ambiguities of my connection to Mormonism, my views have caused deep concern among orthodox members of my family. They are worried about my personal welfare and the future of our family in the next life. I know how deeply that concern is felt. My eight- and ten-year-old daughters believe their daddy isn't a real Mormon and won't go to heaven. No one has told them that directly, but it is a conclusion readily drawn from Primary lessons and sacrament meeting talks. It saddens me that my daughters think their father doesn't measure up.

During the course of my voyages, I have discovered some constellations that have served to guide me. I share them now for whatever value they may have to you.

First is the primacy of personal experience. It is often said that you cannot live on borrowed light. Mormonism even had its genesis in the saying that God gives liberally to all who seek. Subjugating personal experience to the authority of scripture or priesthood leaders is a denial of this fundamental principle. Whether the subjugation is a conscious response to a so-called test of faith or subconscious self-deception, it is a lie. And it is cowardice to live a lie, not humility; and emotional dishonesty to remain willfully ignorant of one's own experience. The time I spend following someone else's star or marching to someone else's drum is time and opportunity lost forever.

Second, I believe that I alone determine the quality of my life. There have been times when life seemed very painful and I felt very inadequate; there have been times when life seemed joyful and I completely competent. The circumstances were not all that different; the difference was how I chose to experience them.

Third, I believe that I am connected to all human beings who are living, have lived, or will live on this earth. And at times I also sense a connection to the earth and the sky, the flowers and the stars. This connection leads me to seek the welfare of others, to celebrate their successes and mourn their losses. As a cultural Mormon, I sometimes feel like a man without a country, but my world has expanded so that I feel more kinship with all of humankind and with the planet we share than I ever did before.

Fourth, I call that which supports and sustains life, which connects and draws us together, God; and I experience God in goodness, truth, and beauty. These virtues are for me inseparable, that which is good being also inherently true and beautiful, and vice versa. In the kingdom of God, truth is not hostage to tradition, beauty does not serve some other purpose, goodness is not contingent on belief. Rather all three have full freedom of expression and are valued in all their diverse manifestations.

Finally my life is fulfilling as long as I am actively pursuing a dream or committed to a specific purpose. In leaving orthodoxy I gave up a ready-made cause that gave my life meaning; I gave up a powerful support system. I have had to define my own dreams, my own reasons for being. That has been difficult, for I am not a skilled creator, but I am working at it.

Jesus is reported to have said, "Ye shall know the truth, and the truth shall make you free." With freedom comes responsibility, not the responsibility of slaves, who have a "duty" to obey their masters, but the responsibility, the opportunity, of the free: to choose, to create, to make a difference in this world. Creation is God's first act. Of all God's people, Mormons, who aspire to become gods, should be creative.

God's second act is reconciliation — sometimes called atonement. Only when I let go of God as commandment-giver, as judge, and embrace a God of love and unconditional forgiveness do I experience reconciliation. When I am forgiving and loving of myself, I am more loving, more forgiving, more available to others.

Unfortunately, although I am a clumsy creator, my attempts at reconciliation often seem downright hopeless. I work at it—but that is
another paper. God's third act is transformation—resurrection, if
you will, and that is also another paper.

For the purposes of this article it is enough to know that I am
the master of my ship, that I am free to choose both my destination
and the quality of the voyage. I am free to sail to faraway lands or
remain safely anchored at the dock. God will not choose for me. I
choose to sail, to sail as far and as widely as I can. Through summer
doldrums and wintry blasts, I am learning to "fear no evil," for God,
hidden and revealed, supports, sustains, and surprises, and makes
life interesting. I am beginning to feel at home at sea.

11.
Another Kind of Faith

Irene M. Bates

ABOUT THREE MONTHS AGO A RELIEF SOCIETY TEACHER PHONED to ask if I would share my testimony of the Book of Mormon in her lesson. I told her I would but that I might not be the right one to ask. I explained that the principles of love taught by Jesus were the foundation of my faith and that where the Book of Mormon illuminates those principles then it serves to build upon that foundation.

There was a pause of a few seconds, and then the teacher asked, "Well then, why do you need to be in the church?" My initial unspoken response was, "Why not?" After all this is the church of Jesus Christ. But as I thought about it I realized her question was relevant. I could be in any Christian church or not even belong to a church if that were indeed the sum total of my interest and faith. Since then I have pondered her question many times.

I know that the foundation of my faith remains deep and strong, yet I also know that over time some of my more naive, idealistic pillars built on that foundation have become somewhat fragile. The kind of saw-edged wisdom that is grief has eroded some quite severely. But I imagine many people have shaky pillars that need shoring up, and it might be more helpful if I shared some of the stalwart supports that have withstood the challenges of the years. Three of them have survived because they are constructed from the materials of my own spiritual experience — those things which I cannot deny. Two are quite predictable and uncomplicated, the third somewhat ironic and complex but always exciting.

First of all, as a convert in a mission setting thirty-three years ago, I was very moved—and still am—by the awakening of the spirit that can be seen in converts. There is a glow, an enrichment of personality, a new kind of self-esteem, a discovery of talent, and a hunger for truth, as well as a touching vulnerability in people as the message of Jesus Christ touches their lives. It has seemed to me that missionaries are like naive angels unaware, who enter the lives of people and mine hidden treasures in the souls of those they teach. I have seen it in many converts and know what that feels like myself. I could tell no end of stories about changed lives—not tales of repentant sinners who become "good" overnight but of people who illumine for me the words of Christ when he said, "I am come that they might have life and that they might have it more abundantly." This is difficult to explain away.

The second support for my faith is a product of the first. Because of that spiritual awakening and the vulnerability accompanying it, we are afforded the opportunity of discovering a deep spiritual kinship with some of our fellow travellers in the church, first with certain missionaries who remain our friends for life and then with others with whom our spirits feel at home. This, too, is difficult to explain away. It is not just a token response, institutionally fostered. It is a spiritual affinity that makes us feel for one another, be responsive to one another, know we can depend on one another. It is, to use Marion D. Hanks's beautiful phrase, an "ultimate concern" that is shared. It can extend to people not of our faith and even to people with whom we do not always agree. It allows for differences.

Not long after we joined the church in England, I read a speech given by Hugh B. Brown at Brigham Young University. It thrilled me when I read it, and it has been a comfort to me since. He said: "We are grateful in the Church and in this great university that the freedom, dignity and integrity of the individual is basic in Church doctrine.... Here we are free to think and express our opinions. Fear will not stifle thought, as is the case in some areas which have not yet emerged from the dark ages."[1] In the mission field there were always differences of opinion openly discussed because there was a hunger for truth, although I admit we did get off the subject at times. I think our present greater preoccupation with order and conformity does a disservice to such vital spiritual exchange. I am reminded of Henry Adams. After touring an art exhibition at the Royal Academy in London, a friend asked Adams what he thought of the show. Adams hesitated and then said he thought it was just chaos really. His friend, Stopford Brooks, answered by asking "whether chaos were not better than death."[2] Lately I have had the sense that our church liberates the spirit only to feel a need to tame it, confine it, and make it conform. This can lead to a loss of vitality of spirit and a fear of honest expression. Nevertheless I cannot deny the wonder of those early experiences and the sense of renewal I always feel, for example, at the Sunstone symposium. I believe the Lord understands my determination to keep alive this spirit of inquiry, to retain the knowledge of what the church can mean in my life. My participation in gatherings of like-minded people provides reinforcement for this particular pillar of my faith.

And this leads me to a third pillar. It may seem a strange one, but from the beginning it has remained deeply rooted despite increasing institutional onslaughts. It has survived, constant and strong, through changes in church leadership and in church policies over the years. It has to do with what I have learned since becoming a member of the church. I don't mean doctrine or scriptures, although they are necessarily a part of it. I mean the significant spiritual insights afforded by having to confront the paradoxes, myths, and contradictions that are ever present in the LDS church. These exist in all institutions, but because of the peculiarities of our faith, they are more accessible for us.

As a lay church we have opportunities to confront and come to terms with the inevitability of conflict and paradox, because most of us are involved in administrative duties as well as spiritual adventures. Choices have to be made in terms of priorities, and there is a constant danger that the element of choice itself may become hidden in institutional routine. A personal experience of mine might serve to illustrate.

My aunt was a staunch Methodist, the soul of integrity, highly practical, not given to displays of emotion, but she had a kind heart which she took pains to disguise. My uncle was not much of a chapel-goer, so when he died my aunt decided to have an informal funeral service in the home. The Methodist minister came and delivered a nice little sermon and then ended with an appropriate prayer. He had barely breathed the word "Amen" when my aunt addressed the group. "Did anyone remember to tell the bread man we don't want any bread today?" That may well have been a cover for emotion, but she *was* very practical.

It seems to me we are faced with that kind of a situation in the church all the time. The practical needs of the institution and the successful implementation of programs and policies require that we attend to such ongoing demands. The programs provide opportunities for growth, but sometimes they become the end rather than the means. I recall not long after we became a stake in Manchester, forever after to be tied to a central bureaucracy, one of our leaders asked my husband if he could be released. He felt he was being swallowed up in paperwork instead of serving as a spiritual leader and comforter, something he felt he had been as a branch president in the mission setting. He feared the ease with which the institutional demands could be allowed to compromise the church's spiritual reason for being. My husband also was keenly aware of that danger. I remember on one occasion after a particularly statistic-oriented stake conference in Salt Lake City, my husband in closing with prayer asked the Lord in all sincerity to help us "feed thy sheep as well as count them." I believe we are all required to be aware of the nature of this ongoing balancing act.

There are other paradoxical concerns. For instance, there is excommunication. In light of the teachings of Jesus, I have always been uncomfortable with the practice of excommunication and disfellowshipping. Despite the rationale given for such actions, it has always seemed to me rather like turning a wounded person away from a hospital lest he leave blood on the clean floor. Where do we draw the line between the need for purity, order, and efficiency in the institution and the aching needs of those individuals the institution is there to serve, those who may need concern and understanding the most? I remember with gratitude Fern Lee, Harold B. Lee's wife. I was being admonished for not regarding the church rules as all important. Sister Lee came to my rescue saying, "Sister Bates, never, ever believe you are required to forget the higher law of kindness." How wonderful it is to experience such elevating incidents firsthand, because often they are the stuff of which myths are made.

And all institutions have myths. They serve a purpose in shaping culture, not least our own Mormon culture, and they are often greater motivators than history. But a church as young as ours, its history relatively accessible, cannot expect those myths to remain unchallenged. It is human nature to seek the elusive truth in history, and history will continue to be rewritten. The church cannot hope to escape revisions in its history, so why not enjoy them and recognize how enriching they can be? Faith itself has to be stronger than history. Joseph Smith's testimony cannot ever be mine. I have to discover my own knowledge and understanding of all truth. Myths may have a purpose—they can be comforting, familiar frameworks for our faith—but that is all they can be. They can never serve as pillars of our faith. They are too vulnerable, I have discovered, and they cannot be allowed to stand guard over truth itself. Since we claim to have the truth, we may be setting ourselves up for a basic contradiction in our faith.

And we have enough contradictions to deal with. The Bible itself has its fair share, and our own prophets have not been im-mune—even contemporary leaders. One General Authority can tell us to turn to the scriptures for guidance, and another caution us to heed the words of current prophets rather than relying on the words of dead prophets. Both can be useful. Both can help us weigh our choices. I know I am quoting a dead prophet, but Brigham Young's advice mediates between those two extremes. He said: "I am more afraid that this people have so much confidence in their leaders that they will not inquire for themselves of God whether they are led by him. I am fearful they settle down in a state of blind self-security, trusting their eternal destiny in the hands of their leaders with a reckless confidence that in itself would thwart the purposes of God in their salvation."[3]

So why do these seeming conflicts reinforce this particular pillar of my faith? It sounds as if they might more appropriately be seen as threats to that faith. At most they might be accepted as a requisite testing of faith by requiring me to endure to the end with-out questioning the inexplicable. The fact is, however, they serve my faith in more positive ways. They do not disturb the foundation of my faith but instead contribute to my understanding of the central purpose of the church in two ways. Ironically, first of all, by requir-ing me to turn to that foundation even more, they bring me closer to the Savior. They cause me to measure everything by the truths Jesus taught and exemplified as I experience the meaning of those principles in my own life. Second, these challenges serve as a means of developing, often painfully, greater understanding, wisdom, and humility. The weighing, the balancing, the choice between two or more competing goods, and the recognition of complexity can help me have compassion for others—even for leaders in their formidable tasks—as I am forced to discover my own values and limitations. When people talk of the simple truths of the gospel, they are right. What more simple teaching than the paramount virtue of love, love of God and love of one's neighbor? What we are less anxious to point out are the complexities involved in living such simple truths.

We talked about this in a book group. A few women from our Relief Society meet once a month in the home of a bright, inquiring woman, who is homebound. At one of our meetings, we discussed what love entailed and how each of us had to interpret what love may require in any given situation. We focused on a specific problem in our ward. Our chapel, which is situated in a lovely secluded area, has been perceived as a relief station by a homeless, mentally disturbed man. He is one of those formerly institutionalized but now out on his own. We discussed the differences of opinion which have emerged informally in our ward as to how true caring might be expressed in his case. And I recognized anew how truly Lowell Bennion spoke when he pointed to the necessity of loving intelligently with a knowledge of human nature and its needs. In the case of the homeless man, we gave him food, allowed him to use the bathroom facilities at church, but when the bishop tried to get help for him he left.

The organizational structure of our church can afford us access to the paradoxes, myths, and contradictions of our faith in ways which many religions, given the nature of their structures, do not. The ultimate irony is that although the church preaches simple ideas and standards and rather simplistic prescriptions for living them, in practice it contributes its own share of contradictions and in so doing affords us the opportunity to grow and develop spiritual insights. It is true that some choose not to notice troubling questions. But my experience in the church over the years has taught me that when we do confront these challenges we become alive in a faith which is truly our own. We suffer the pain and uncertainty, take the risks, and enjoy the exhilaration of personal discovery.

The "wisdom of age," I believe, has less to do with such experience than the kind of honesty and courage and trust shown by a small son of friends of mine. One day while riding in the car with his mother, he said, "Mom, I don't think God can be perfect." She asked why he thought that. And he answered, "Well, in the Old Testament it tells of God sending the Israelites to kill people. They were all his children. Good parents don't kill their own children."

That is quite an observation for a nine-year-old boy. I think God must have a special love for that pure, trusting, and concerned spirit. I hope well-meaning members will not discourage Jeff's honesty. I know his parents won't. It may seem a small incident, but it touched me very deeply, and I wondered why. Later as I thought about it again and again, I realized that there in that one small boy was manifest a central pillar of my faith. He had dared to face God honestly and without fear. In so doing he reaffirmed the promise of the gospel in my own life. Love itself was ever present for me before joining the church. Conversion simply widened the lens. But this new and significant aspect of faith was awakened in me. Since my conversion, there has been — to use the words of Elizabeth Barrett Browning — an "ever-lasting face-to-face with God"[4] in my ongoing search for truth. In an institutional setting such a quest can be quite perilous and frustrating at times. In gatherings of people who share the quest, one can emerge unafraid. On a personal level it is both humbling and inspiring. And it is always exciting.

NOTES

1. Hugh B. Brown, "An Address Delivered at Brigham Young University," 29 March 1958.

2. Henry Adams, *The Education of Henry Adams* (New York: Modern Library, 1931), 220.

3. Brigham Young, *Discourses of Brigham Young*, ed. John A. Widtsoe (Salt Lake City: Deseret Book, 1954), 135.

4. Elizabeth Barrett Browning, *The Poetical Works of Elizabeth Barrett Browning* (London: Oxford University Press, 1908), 333.

12.
A Christian by Yearning

Levi S. Peterson

I BELONG TO A LARGE AND AFFECTIONATE FAMILY. THROUGH phone calls, letters, and reunions, I keep in touch with brothers, sisters, nephews, nieces, and innumerable cousins, most of whom are faithful Latter-day Saints. I converse amicably with my relatives on many subjects. However, when I take up the topic of religion, they often become wary and reserved. They know I am a doubter, and they wish to avoid an unseemly confrontation.

I acknowledge that it is my own provocative and ribald behavior that places a barrier between me and my relatives. That fact does not diminish my regret, for I love them very much. On occasion I suffer from the perception that I am dangerous to them. I am like Rappaccini's daughter in Hawthorne's famous story. The unearthly flowers which the scientist Rappaccini had created imbued his daughter with a lethal emanation. She could not associate with ordinary mortals because her very breath would kill them. As I say, I find in Hawthorne's story an apt figure for my relationship with those faithful Mormons who hold me in greatest affection. At times I feel my mere presence is a poison.

Four or five years ago, my sister, Mary, surprised me by confiding to me a spiritual manifestation she had experienced in the Mesa temple. I see Mary only once or twice a year on my visits to Arizona. She always greets me with a warm embrace and chats affably about our mutual concerns. Yet I believe she feels vulnerable and cautiously avoids challenges to her faith. With many apologies she returned unread a book of my short stories which I had mailed her as a gift. I therefore recognized an extraordinary courage and generosity when she shared with me her remarkable experience with deity. I think she risked my rebuttal and scorn, which I am happy to say I neither felt nor expressed, because she hoped to help me. I think she hoped the unusual manifestation given her would help turn me toward a more complete obedience to the commandments.

When I was a child I both believed and doubted. When my brothers told me God's eyes could pierce concrete or could penetrate the dark recesses of a root cellar where I had taken refuge to pursue unhallowed impulses, I doubted that they could. On the other hand, I often found myself directing silent sentences toward God as if I truly believed that he had hid himself within the sound of my imagined voice. Now that I am an adult, I no longer hold conversations with God. I am too much a doubter, having no gift for intuiting spirit beyond the world of matter. Yet I am still a Christian and a Latter-day Saint. To many my Christian aspirations will seem paltry. I have no thoughts about exaltation in the celestial kingdom, no ambitions to be a king, priest, and ruler over worlds without end. Instead I concentrate upon the most incredible miracle, the resurrection of the dead. I will thank my Lord with an utter fervor if he will again give form and fire to my cold ashes.

I became a doubter within a few days after my arrival in the French mission in November 1954. Late one afternoon my senior companion and I arrived in La Chaux de Fonds, a small watchmaking city in the Jura Mountains of Switzerland. Without pause we deposited our trunks in our new quarters and conscientiously went out tracting. For a couple of hours we knocked on doors without gaining entrance. In that brief period I reassessed the nature of my mission. Its novelty and achievement had already faded and its tedium and frustration loomed. Clearly the vast majority of people in the world were apathetic toward the Latter-day Saint message. I was therefore doubly grateful when at last a man invited us in. Although his bristling grey hair and round wire-rimmed spectacles gave him a stern, ascetic appearance, he seated us with polite dignity and asked his wife to serve us mint tea and cookies. He informed us that he favored the Jehovah's Witnesses but would value any new light we might throw upon the Bible. He listened attentively and scrutinized each biblical passage to which we referred. He agreed that we could return on another day and again on another. At the end of our third meeting he politely said he had heard enough. He could not find sufficient evidence for the Joseph Smith story in his Bible to justify further lessons.

This turn of events, minor though it was, precipitated a spiritual crisis for me. According to the faith in which I had been raised, this man stood condemned. He could make no excuse on Judgment Day. He could not claim that the missionaries had failed to reach him and that the glad tidings had never been preached to him. He had examined the truth closely yet had denied it. This was a crisis, I say, because I simply could not believe that a man of such evident kindness and sincerity could stand in any manner condemned before God. And by extension I had suddenly lost my ability to believe that all the other good and sincere people in the world would stand condemned for failing to accept the particular interpretation of the gospel which the Mormon missionaries carried. It no longer seemed imperative to me that everyone in the world become a Latter-day Saint. And with the fall of this premise, a long line of other premises tumbled like dominoes in my mind.

I do not need to say that my mission proved a difficult experience. At one moment after I had been made a senior companion and transferred to Charleroi, Belgium, I made arrangements to abandon my mission and only at the last moment decided to carry on, principally because I couldn't think of a single person who would welcome me home. I knocked on thousands of doors and delivered the missionary lessons hundreds of times in a strictly matter-of-fact, expository vein. I refused to bear a testimony, and I lived with a constant dread that someone might ask me point blank whether I believed what I preached. Luckily no one ever did. I baptized three persons and was the initial contact for a family who later proved, as most converts in those days did not, permanent, sustaining members of their branch. In addition I regularly saved a third to a half of my monthly stipend and gave it to the poor I met while tracting, and I used my beloved Louis Segond translation of the Bible to comfort and encourage the downhearted I met in any context, regardless of their attitude toward the Latter-day Saint message. A Mormon missionary could be, I learned, a kind of roving free-lance minister of the universal gospel. It now seems, thirty-one years following my return, that my mission was a rare and invaluable experience and that I am fortunate to have been persuaded to carry it to an honorable end.

Today I am a more or less active Mormon. I attend sacrament meeting regularly, I am a home teacher, I am a substitute instructor of my ward high priests' group. I am uninterested in what I will call secondary theological questions such as the authenticity of the Book of Mormon, the prophetical character of Joseph Smith, and the doctrine of three degrees of glory. I do not quarrel with those doctrines. If my fellow Mormons consider them important, I too will stand by them, and I will certainly not fail to give them an orthodox cast when I lead discussions in my high priests' group. But in my private ruminations I dwell instead upon the more primary matters of the parenthood of God, the redemptive sacrifice of Jesus Christ, and the immortality of the human soul.

Predictably I sense that my worship differs from that of many with whom I share a pew in sacrament meeting. This difference arises, I think, from a difference in the focus of our fundamental human anxiety. Christians have traditionally been anxious chiefly over the salvation of their soul. I speak here of salvation in the broad Christian usage signifying the entrance of the soul after death into the bliss of God's eternal presence. The late medieval English play *Everyman* expresses this traditional anxiety in a forthright manner. At the beginning of this simple allegory, God commands Death to summon Everyman before him for judgment. When Death informs Everyman that he must descend into the grave, this representative of universal humanity frantically begs time to arrange his affairs. Death allows him only to canvass his acquaintances to determine who will accompany him into the grave. Everyman is greatly disillusioned to discover that, despite their earlier promises, his hearty comrades Fellowship, Kindred, and Goods refuse to go with him. Even his old allies Strength, Discretion, Beauty, and Five Wits ultimately fail to accompany him. Only Good Deeds, much attenuated by Everyman's long neglect, is willing to go with him to judgment. As the play ends and Everyman and Good Deeds, newly fortified by Knowledge and Confession, descend into the grave, Everyman prays: "Into thy hands, Lord, my soul I commend. Receive it, Lord, that it be not lost. As thou me boughtest, so me defend. And save me from the fiend's boast, That I may appear with that blessed host, That shall be saved at the day of doom."

Although Latter-day Saints assert that their theology has abolished the doctrine of hell, they actually fear eternal punishment in much the same manner as other Christians. The outer darkness to which Mormons relegate those who deny the Holy Ghost is in its own way as frightening as the fiery hell in which their Puritan ancestors believed. Of course Mormons commonly reassure one another that most sinners will be assigned to the lesser kingdoms of glory, the telestial and terrestrial kingdoms. These kingdoms are not thought of as places of active torment; their inhabitants will suffer chiefly because they will recognize the infinite opportunities of the celestial kingdom which they have failed to inherit. The blessed inhabitants of the celestial kingdom will enjoy the presence of God and will become the creators of worlds and the parents of spiritual children. As benign as this teaching seems, the prospect of failing to achieve the celestial kingdom fills many Latter-day Saints with dread. Even faithful, meticulous Mormons frequently express anxiety that they will not prove worthy of that blissful condition. In effect they suffer a traditional Christian anxiety over damnation.

If I differ from the typical Latter-day Saint, it is because my anxiety is focused not upon whether my immortal soul may suffer damnation but upon whether I have an immortal soul. I find my anxiety well expressed in *The Seventh Seal*, a movie by Swedish director Ingmar Bergman. I have viewed this movie numerous times during the past thirty years. Like *Everyman*, this movie is an allegory. It is about a medieval knight who encounters Death while returning from a crusade. Whimsically Death agrees to a game of chess, to be played intermittently as the knight and his companions ride cross-country toward the knight's castle. As long as the knight can forestall the checkmating of his king, Death will allow him to live. Everywhere are grisly reminders of Death's dominion, for the plague is sweeping the land. An entire village has been decimated; an unburied corpse rots by the roadside; a villainous priest dies in agony before the horrified eyes of the knight and his retinue. Furthermore, the knight is a doubter consumed by the question of whether God exists and, contingently, whether the human soul will persist beyond the grave. At one point he asks a young witch who is being burned at the stake whether she has truly had commerce with Satan, since the existence of Satan would imply the existence of God. Her ambiguous reply gives him no satisfaction, and her cruel demise only exacerbates his anxiety. His questions remain unanswered. As the movie closes, Death claims the knight and his companions, leading them in a *danse macabre* across a distant skyline.

Like the knight of *The Seventh Seal*, I fear that the human soul evaporates with death. I live in anxiety of annihilation, and this anxiety conditions the nature of my worship. I will not argue that my kind of worship is better than or even equal to the worship of conventional Mormons. I will argue, however, that it merits consideration. It seems to me that I respond to Christian meanings which many others ignore. As paradoxical as it may seem, there are religious advantages to doubt.

One advantage of doubt is the perspective it offers upon the rite of the Lord's Last Supper, to which Mormons give the distinguishing title of the *sacrament*. The prayers of the sacrament enjoin participants to remember the mutilated body and spilled blood of the crucified Lord and to obey his commandments in order to have his spirit to be with them. The Latter-day Saints observe a reverent silence during the sacrament, making it a period of meditation and recollectedness. Although I can't know with certainty what my fellow worshippers meditate upon, I believe that most of them contemplate their successes and failures in living a Christian life. They do this because the church has chosen to emphasize the sacrament as a renewal of one's vows to live righteously. The Latter-day Saints are, as my priesthood lesson manual informs me, a covenant-making people who perpetually refresh their commitment to obey God's commandments by partaking of the sacrament. I trust that for most Mormons the renewal of this commitment is a propitious and rejuvenating experience. Undoubtedly they yield themselves to God's designs and rejoice in the sheltering sweep of his providence. Perhaps they contemplate the agonies of the Lord on the cross and experience gratitude for the redemptive sacrifice which effaces the desperate consequences of their sins and opens before them the stairway to glory.

Often as I partake of the sacrament, I vicariously borrow a like response from my fellow worshippers. As the deacons distribute the bread and water, I think about my baptism long ago in an icy creek and about the obligation of obedience that even at the age of eight I understood myself to be under. Moreover, I imagine myself to be contrite over my infractions of the commandments and resolute about mastering my imperfections. Finally, however, I return to my private reality. This is not my own true response to the rite of the Lord's Last Supper.

For about ten years following my mission, on those infrequent occasions when I attended church, I partook of the sacrament from motives that seemed strictly social. I partook of it in order not to disturb the meditations of my neighbors by rousing their curiosity as to my reasons for not partaking of it. When our daughter turned three, my wife and I agreed that she should be raised a Mormon, and we began to attend meetings with greater regularity. It did not take me long to recognize that I responded to the sacrament with an apprehensive grief. Often I had to halt my singing during the sacrament hymn and clench my teeth in order not to weep. In time a curious symbolism grew on me. During each service the sacrament table and its plates of bread and trays of water sat before the congregation covered by a white satin cloth. Irresistibly I identified the sacrament table with my father's coffin. When my father died when I was nine, a local craftsman constructed a coffin and Relief Society sisters covered it with white satin. During the funeral the coffin sat immediately in front of the congregation.

Unquestionably the sacrament had become a tragic ceremony for me. Its tragic meanings, of course, ranged far beyond the connection I made between my father's coffin and the particular setting of the sacrament table in my ward. Its tragic meaning derived from nothing less than the premise that God himself in the person of Jesus Christ suffered and died. Even the faithful are sobered by the contemplation that Christ endured an agony so vast that it could redeem the sins of an entire world and that he lapsed, if only momentarily, into the cold immobility of death. But, of course, the faithful are sheltered from utter grief by their belief in the resurrection. The Lord's Last Supper has always been taken as a symbol of hope. According to the account of its first occurrence, Jesus broke bread and poured wine for his apostles and expressly urged them to remember him. He had given them a tangible sign of his transcendent reality. It would remind them in the dark times of his absence that he had risen and would return. But for me, doubting alike Jesus' immortality and my own, the sacrament seemed an adumbration of despair, a weekly reminder that bright landscapes and beloved personalities from my past were irretrievably lost.

Time has elapsed and I have become even more consistent in attending meetings and performing my minor ecclesiastical duties. My response to the sacrament has evolved or at least has enlarged and become more complex. Often when I partake of the bread and water my mood is such that I ignore the benumbing possibility that human destiny is eternal death. Instead I contemplate the egregious, absurd, astonishing, miraculous proposition that on a certain resplendent morning the graves of all history will open and the incarcerated dead, one and all, will emerge into a new and everlasting life. In such a mood I allow my imagination to construct a Christian future. I pay no heed to the conjecture of my associates about the furnishings of the resurrected world. I reject out of hand an earth transfigured by glory like a sea of glass. Furthermore, I pay no heed to the belief of many that because of my perversity I will be denied the presence of God and my loved ones. If I have surrendered to a miracle, I insist that it be an entire miracle. On the morning of the resurrection I will greet my wife, my daughter, my father and mother, my brothers and sisters, and a host of other dear relatives and friends, as I knew them in the finest moments of their mortality, clothed as I once knew them, speaking as I once heard them. Around them I will see the friendly surface of the earth as I once knew it, broad and fair with plains and mountains, forests and rivers, farms, villages, and cities. And soon I will see the architect of this miracle threading his way among the crowds of the resurrected, speaking kindly, giving reassurances, recognizing all as if indeed he has had with each a long and perfect familiarity. His countenance will be radiant with grace.

I am a Christian by yearning. Opposed to my doubt and perversity is a longing that the gospel be true. Christians are made, said the apostle Paul, of faith, hope, and charity. Though I have little charity and less faith, perhaps I have hope in some abundance. Often when I recognize how intensely I yearn for eternal life, I find myself elevated and encouraged. I find that my yearning has transformed itself into hope and I find myself responding to the sacrament as a ceremony of hope. On many Sundays while I participate in this solemn ritual, I ponder the possibility that Christ will one day resurrect me, and I am filled with gratitude that such a thing might come to pass.

When I attended a family reunion in Arizona a little more than a year ago, I found my brother Arley absent. His sons reported him to be very frail and ailing. When the reunion was over, I drove to Mesa and on an early evening dropped in on Arley. He made his way from the supper table to an easy chair with trembling legs, and he sat with his shoulders so slumped and his head so drooped that I wondered whether his chin would touch his knees. I asked him questions about our father and about our father's first wife, Arley's mother, and about the penurious homestead they had struggled to develop. Narrating anecdotes from the family's past, Arley seemed invigorated and greatly pleased. I too was greatly pleased. We each discerned in the other a vital trace of our father. For a couple of hours there in Arley's Mesa home, we evoked our father's pulsing, blooming presence.

At leave taking I gripped Arley's hand and hugged his frail shoulders. It was an extraordinary goodbye. I feared, with good reason as it turned out, that he would die before I saw him again. A sense of the sacred accompanied me as I left his house and walked toward the home of my sister Mary, where I would spend the night. My way led past the Mesa temple. It was dark and the temple was illuminated. I remembered that the temple is a holy place, and I remembered that I had just come from a holy place, a living room made sacred by the fervent goodbye of two brothers. I spoke to Mary when I arrived at her house. Mary had been at the reunion and had returned early to Mesa largely for my convenience. I stood with her at her kitchen sink while she tidied up a few dishes. I said a person could find the sacred in places other than a temple. I said holiness is as wild and free as the air. It circulates everywhere. I have felt it often in the presence of the newborn and the dead. I have felt it in a sunrise or along a mountain stream. In a soft voice Mary agreed. She said she too had met the sacred in unexpected places. Then we fell silent, each cherishing the proximity of the other.

People who have known each other for a lifetime can abruptly resume a topic of conversation after years of leaving it dormant. At her kitchen sink I renewed the discussion Mary had opened when she shared with me her sacred experience in the temple. My literal words concealed a larger meaning. Mary had loved me enough to share a sacred experience in hopes it would give me faith. I loved her enough now to share a sacred experience so that she would at least know that I am not irreligious. I think that was all I meant to say, and perhaps it was enough for the moment. Months or perhaps years from now I will renew my dialogue with Mary, and I will tell her how I feel about the resurrection when I partake of the sacrament. I do not know how I will persuade her not to worry over my poor prospects on Judgment Day. But perhaps she will be comforted to know that even a doubter can hope.

If Christ has indeed purchased eternal life for humanity, I for one will awaken to the reality of his gift with an immeasurable gratitude. In the meantime I make it the center of my Christian worship to anticipate that gratitude when I partake of the sacrament. I do not belittle the communion of my fellow Mormons. It is not an unworthy way of celebrating the Lord's Last Supper to measure one's successes and failures in keeping the commandments and to renew one's covenants to live righteously. Yet in a sense it seems a pity to take one's immortality for granted, to expect it and count on it. It seems a pity to be so sheltered from the terror of death that one's gratitude for the resurrection is merely dutiful and perfunctory. Perhaps truly there are religious advantages to doubt. Perhaps only a doubter can appreciate the miracle of life without end.

13.
Respite for a Heretic: Jesus Christ and the Language of Desire

Donlu DeWitt Thayer

I HAVE LIVED MY WHOLE LIFE IN A DISSOLVING WORLD, THOUGH for a long time this did not matter to me much. The year I was born Richard M. Weaver published his book, *Ideas Have Consequences*. This was, Weaver said, "another book about the dissolution of the West," a process he traces to a change in metaphors for comprehending and shaping reality which occurred in the fourteenth century when William of Occam and the nominalists won the great medieval debate over the existence of universals. When humanity ceased to believe in the reality of universals, says Weaver, it made an evil decision, which began the "abomination of desolation" that appears in the modern world as a "feeling of alienation from fixed truth."[1]

But I grew up in a different history. Instructed in and measured against truths that were fixed, that were the word of God revealed through holy books and prophets living and dead, I was certain of everything that really mattered—of God and his son Jesus Christ, of the Mormon church and its inspired programs, of the universe and my place in it. Of course I knew of the evil world outside whence could come atom bombs or evil people and of the natural world where accident and disease could maim and kill. But the point of life was to overcome the world, to fight our way to our true home, where God (Father and Mother) and Christ dwell.

We could do this by following carefully the sure guides. I could follow those guides, for I was not just any ordinary person; I was a youth of noble birthright, stalwart and brave, firm as the mountains around me, a member of the chosen generation saved for these latter days. I was glad that I would be punished for my own sins and not for Adam's (or Eve's) transgression. I was in a word special.

All through my childhood I lived in expectation of some miraculous confirmation of my own particular spiritual prodigiousness. For a while when I was very young, I thought that perhaps I would somehow confound the wise in the temple at age eleven-and-a-half. More likely though I would have a vision, a revelation from God that would reveal to me a secret of godliness and tell me the great and unique task set for me in mortality.

By the time I was fourteen, I had begun to worry that it wasn't good to think I was so special. I made up a little slogan that I hoped would remind me to be better. I wrote it down and posted it where I could see it every day: "Some people need to know God loves them. Other people need to know God loves other people too." I tended, I knew, to be the second kind of person. I didn't know what to do about this.

Of course I knew I had faults. And I strove to purge myself of weakness and sin, setting goals, keeping lists, certifying my spot in the ranks of the chosen. I hadn't had a vision in time to be special in the way Joseph Smith was, but maybe there would be something else. Perhaps I could become the mother of the great prophet of the last days. I didn't think about this very often though. I had other things on my mind. The trials of adolescence broke my attention, got in the way of my clear thoughts about the secrets of godliness. And so I missed it. For now I realize that in a much less dramatic way than I had expected, I had received my vision at the very time I had been expecting it. When I was moved at age fourteen to write that little slogan, I had received the most important revelation of my life. But it would be a long time before I would understand the love of God for other people.

Yes I had my faults, and I could work on those systematically until I was perfect. But there was nothing basically, fundamentally wrong with me, with my ideas. I *knew* that if everyone could see and feel as I did, the world would be good and safe. I was almost twenty years old before the Vietnam War and my feeble attempts to discuss it with French communists in student restaurants in Grenoble brought me my first real anxiety about my own fallibility, about threats to my ideological security from the "outside world." Here were people, seemingly sane and happy, who had never heard of Joseph Smith, who were confident of truth as they saw it. I knew they must be wrong, but I couldn't refute their arguments. I decided to feel sorry for them, and I took up eating strawberry tarts in *patisseries* instead of talking to communists at lunch.

I gained fifteen pounds and went home to Utah where the world would be safe and right again. But I discovered that I was no longer safe, not even here. I had seen something that I could not stop seeing. I know now that disillusionment is a natural part of maturing. It clears the mind for the new vision of experience. In some societies disenchantment is built into the rituals of a religious education: the Zen initiate must endure the broken Buddha; the Hopi youth sees the unmasking of the Kachina. This is meant to shock the young person into "grasping a higher reality" and developing a "mature religious perspective."[2] But as far as I could tell, my disillusionment was not orchestrated or guided, and I felt betrayed.

As the evidence mounted against the "establishment," I began to turn my criticism more and more upon those who seemed to reach adulthood without ever knowing that anything was *wrong*. The church, for instance, seemed full of grown-up children, people who could still believe in being special and right, people who could still be happy being the way I used to be. These people were blind and foolish. They were not to be tolerated. So now my world was full of stereotypes—"us," careful-thinking deeply spiritual followers of Jesus Christ, and "them," narrow-minded, sentimental, materialistic members of the Mormon Club. "They" were the true heretics. They were the ones who were hanging the living gospel up on the goalpost to die, whose behaviorist agendas were turning the bread of life, staled by overexposure, into misguided and pointless programs. It seemed to me that the fountains of living waters were clogged with discarded checklists. I wondered that people would not look up from their statistics or down from their worldly successes and *live*.

But I was not living. I was dying. I could not see that in my critical heart I was still preoccupied with "specialness," that I was jockeying with those I criticized for evidence of God's favor. Preoccupied with the contributions of others to my pain, I was unable to learn how to find what could really help me. I was irritable, lonely, needy, sad. I alienated friends with my attitudes; my family suffered. Finally, like a spoiled child who cannot force the world to do her will, I was in an almost perpetual despairing rage.

So, estranged from reality, I began to feel that nothing was real except the pain of my neediness. I did not know then that my needs were fictions and that neediness itself was part of my sin. So when in dark days of despair I would ask God to take away my pain, to carry me across the abyss, the "silence" did not mean that God was refusing to rescue me because I was supposed to suffer, as if suffering in itself were good for me. The silence meant rather that even God could not take away something I was creating—the emptiness of the refusal to be filled. God could not carry me "through" something that was an illusion, but could only teach me to see more clearly, and only if I would turn to heaven and open my eyes. God could only fill me with love if I would open my heart to receive.

Gaining a path to health was not easy. I knew that it was necessary, but I was reluctant for the real work. It was easier sometimes to endure the accustomed pain than it was to change old habits of mind. For some time, predictably enough, I worked to name my problem precisely, so that I could control it. I read dozens of psychology books, religion books, philosophy books, so that I could more perfectly comprehend what was wrong with me. Each new insight was opportunity for analysis, rationalization, explanation, accusation. But at last I was exhausted from this vain obsession with myself and my emotions.

The beginning of change for me was marked in my mind by the memory of an afternoon when a friend spoke to me the words of Jesus from John 15: "As the Father hath loved me, so I have loved you: continue ye in my love. . . . These things have I spoken unto you that your joy might be full. This is my commandment. That ye love one another, as I have loved you. Greater love hath no man than this, that a man lay down his life for his friends. Ye are my friends if ye do whatsoever I command you. Henceforth I call you not servants; for the servant knoweth not what his lord doeth: but I have called you friends; for all things that I have heard of my Father I have made known unto you."

These familiar words of Jesus pierced my heart as they were spoken to me by someone who loved me and who also loved everyone else he knew. Until that moment I had denied the importance of this affection arising from my friend's own virtue not my "specialness," free for everyone, not unique for me and therefore, I thought, meaningless. But in that moment I knew that my friend, like Jesus to his disciples, was giving me all he knew. He loved me; he wanted to help me; he would not be more "special" than I. And so a seed of virtue was planted in my heart. As it grew it would first break my heart and then heal it.

I desperately wanted to know how to live virtuous, whole, joyful, and I prayed for clearer sight, for knowledge of how to stop the pain I caused myself and others. In vivid dreams I saw rehearsed real moments from my life. I saw myself over and over again— self-absorbed, competitive, critical, manipulative. I heard myself speak, knew the effects of my behavior on others, my friends. At the same time I saw my heart and the hearts of my friends. I saw that sometimes I had taken offense when none had been given; sometimes I had criticized unjustly. I saw myself miserable and lonely because of what I had done. I was filled with sorrow.

This sorrow was much different from the black, static, self-regarding pain of my despair. This sorrow was grief for those I had wronged, including strangely enough the "self" I watched suffer in these scenes. I was sorry not so much that I had done something wrong as that I had done injury to others, to myself, to God. At the same time I saw that sometimes my heart had been right. Sometimes I had been tolerant and patient; sometimes I had given all I had and all I knew; sometimes I had absorbed offense with love; sometimes I had been a friend. Seeing this filled me with joy.

This was what I had needed to see: my own actions creating my own sorrow and my own joy. I was being instructed from my own experience in how to be, and I was receiving a new sense of God's love. It was not out of neediness that God loved me, the human smothering, insistent desire to possess, to convince, to be completed, vindicated, affirmed. Rather it was a strong, clear desire from wholeness, not desire of me from him for his glory but desire for me *as* his glory. It was a desire independent of my desirability, unchanged by my unworthiness. In my competitive heart it had seemed that such a love would be meaningless. If I was not loved for my merits, how could it mean anything? But now I saw that this love, the pure love of Christ, was the only meaning there is.

Such love in every human heart would stop the dissolution, would heal the entire world. It seemed obvious to me now that while attraction, evoked by attributes that can change, often fails, the pure love of Christ can never fail. It is not blind to faults, but there is no self-interest in its discernment of the failings of others. It seeks life and light for all.

In feeling this love, this desire for me, I felt regarded by God, seen, called by my name. I saw that he did not descend below all things in order to remain forever remote from the struggling crea- ture below. He descended in order to be with me, so that I could be with him. Seeing this I understood at last what people are for: they are to be with in their sorrow and in their joy. The purpose of love, its "work and glory," is to bring to pass immortality and eternal life for others. To be possessed of this love is to participate in the order of the universe. Failing this, regardless of our other gifts, we are nothing, which thing I had never really supposed.

Recently I learned that the word "sin" is etymologically re- lated to the verb "to be." It suggests incomplete being, that which is unfinished, not whole.[3] All have sinned and come short of the glory of God. This does not mean that we have not yet finished doing everything on the Great Checklist of Life. It means that we lack perfect love—the desire, the will, the ability to create, to bring light and life to the world; we are alienated from Truth. This alienation creates a sense of neediness.

But we can learn love. Desiring earnestly, praying with "all the energy" of our hearts, we can receive this best of all gifts from a gracious God. Knowing love we are freed from the futility of egocen- tric striving to root out our own imperfections. God's gracious gift is not his loving; love is his very nature, which he cannot hide or withhold. His gift is the Way to *our* loving. His gift is his Word, his Son, his Perfect Love. Receiving Jesus, and so learning this love, can sustain through fear of failing, fear of the opinions of other, fear of wrong ideas, fear of loss or betrayal or rejection.

God does not promise a life free from sorrow. In this world we will always have tribulation, but Perfect Love has "overcome the world" and will if we allow cast out all our fear. So my repentance is not an accomplishment; it is a way of life, a state of mind. I know I must continue to choose, turning and returning my wandering heart to love, accepting chastening when it comes, learning grace upon grace how to be a friend to Jesus Christ. I find there is always room to be a more loving wife, a more consistently patient mother, a better friend. I find I even enjoy church meetings more now too. Instead of mentally murmuring my way through the travelogues and bursts of speculative theology in testimony meetings, I regard the members of the congregation tolerantly, wondering if anything that I am able to give could be needed by them.

I am also more careful now than I used to be of facile distinctions between the church and the gospel. I am more careful when I can remember my resolve and put "myself" aside, of what I say about the church and its members and leaders. I do not see in the church the kind of perfection I once thought it *must* have, but I do see opportunity to find embodiment of the only idea that really matters—that love is everything. By subjecting myself as the spirit directs to the requirements of membership in the church, I can learn to bridle my pride, my anger, my impatience, my irritability, so that I might be filled with love. I learn in the church as I do in marriage, in parenthood, in friendship, in teaching, in writing, in the beauty of my rose garden, that subjection of the will to a strenuous form can bring unexpected rewards. In the keeping of covenants—of baptism, of priesthood, of endowment, of the holy order of matrimony—the order in our individual lives reaches out into the community of faith. I cannot stop the world's dissolving, cannot prevent the evil that comes my way, except as I can bring order to my own heart, receiving there the desire of Jesus Christ, the gracious gift made by one who emptied himself (the literal rendering of Philippians 2:7) of his glory to be born, suffer, and die so that I might if I would be filled.

The ability to be filled comes from, as one Christian psychologist has put it, "our learning how to receive our being in the feminine way, at the wounded core. It comes from our acknowledging our dependency of being-one-with others."[4] This leads us to discover that "we want to be with what matters most to us, with what gives life to any and all being. No longer satisfied with substitute sensations of being we pursue inspection of who we really are and who others really are in all their differences and samenesses to us."[5]

Receiving "being," knowledge, substance, truth in this way (which Ann Ulanov calls "feminine" and which might also be called the Hebrew mode) is an action of the heart that we all, male as well as female, neglect at our peril. The "proclaiming rhetoric of the Bible,"

says Northrop Frye, "is a welcoming and approaching rhetoric, addressed by a symbolically male God to a symbolically female body of
readers": "The 'word of God' is described in the New Testament as a
two-edged sword that cuts and divides. . . . What it ultimately divides
is . . . the world of life and the world of death, and this can be
accomplished only by a language that escapes from argument and
refutation . . . in short, the language of love."[6]

The language of love calls us from the death of our neediness into the abundant life. By submitting our lives to direction by a
will higher than our own, we learn within the bounds the Lord has
set a divine economy. Need is "an economy of scarcity," of poverty,
while desire is "an economy of abundance."[7] It is the abundance of a
pure heart that is seen in such friends of God as Enos or as the
Nephite disciples who learned a language of prayer beyond mortal
ability to describe, or as Joseph Smith, who said that "the nearer we
get to our Heavenly Father, the more we are disposed to look with
compassion upon perishing souls; we feel that we want to take them
upon our shoulders and cast their sins behind our backs."[8]

I would like to be such a friend to Jesus. I have seen that his
desire for my friendship is greater than any desire I have ever
known. Seeing this has brought me to the ability to imagine such a
friendship. Too often, however, my compassion extends only to "perishing souls" who are appealing—who are very young, very old, or
are disadvantaged, hurt, shabby, disabled, or oppressed. For others
who "perish," such as those who are self-righteous, who are blind to
real spiritual truth, or who are in other ways boring or inconvenient,
it is still difficult for me consistently to feel real compassion. I tend
still to long for the Lord to cleanse his church of my ideological foes
and so bring Zion.

Recently, however, I found the following statement from
Brigham Young: "Do not be too anxious for the Lord to hasten his
work. Let our anxiety be centered upon this one thing, the sanctifi-
cation of our own hearts, the purifying of our own affections. This
should be our concern, this should be our study, this should be our
daily prayer, and not be in a hurry to see the overthrow of the
wicked."[9] So I set myself once more to the task of purifying this heart
so prone to wander from the Word of God. It is not, I have to say,
always clear to me what to do. The Way is not so well defined as life
seemed when I was young and sure of everything. I can see at least

that unity with others is essential to personal wholeness and union with God and that such unity does not imply complete agreement of ideas. It does imply, however, mutual desire for wholeness, and this requires a mentality of forgiving. Of me it is required to forgive all offense, for in the end all offense is offense only to God and can only be judged by him. There is no harm in offense except to the one who offends and the one who will "take offense." "For in nothing doth man offend God . . . save [he] confess not his hand in all things, and obey not his commandments" (D&C 59:21), which commandments are circumscribed in love. The great metaphor for unity is the body of Christ; we are all members and have need of each other. It seems to me, however, that "metaphors of unity and integration take us only so far, because they are derived from the finiteness of the human mind. If we are to expand our vision into the genuinely infinite, that vision becomes decentralized. We follow a 'way' or direction until we reach a state of innocence symbolized by the sheep in the twenty-third psalm, where we are back to wandering, but where wandering no longer means being lost."[10]

Though I "wander" a good deal these days, less certain now than I have been before, I am also more serene and less afraid. Perhaps, though I wander, I am now more often safely in the Way of Truth.

Yet life does not often seem any simpler. My new understanding does not relieve me of the responsibility to evaluate, to discern, to make decisions that are painful to me and distressing to others. I cannot do all that pleases everyone who is touched by my life. I know that even if I do right, I will inevitably be the means by which offenses come to others. I will watch others estrange themselves from me. I will only be able to trust that what I try to do in purity of heart will be enough and that what I inevitably do in sin will not be too much. And I will try to avoid receiving offense. The One who calls to me has taken upon himself all offense, and I must accept his work.

So while this life is not simple, the yoke of Christ is easy, and his burden is light. Wandering then, I listen for his call so that I do not fear too much and lose the way. Shepherd, king, bridegroom, host, mother, father, friend—he calls in many voices, all one voice. He calls and waits that I should hear and come with desire. Make ready for the bridegroom; the bridegroom comes. How often I would have gathered you as a hen gathers her chicks, and you would not. Come unto me, all you that labor and are heavy laden, and I will give you rest. Take my yoke upon you and learn of me, for I am meek and lowly in heart: and you shall find rest unto your souls. Fear not, little children, for you are mine. Be of good cheer, and do not fear. In my Father's house are many mansions. If it were not so I would have told you. I go to prepare a place for you. And if I go and prepare a place for you, I will come again and receive you unto myself, that where I am there you may be also. And where I go you know, and the way you know. I am the way, the truth, and the life. He that believes in me, though he were dead, yet shall he live. In this world you shall have tribulation. But fear not: I have overcome the world. This is my work and my glory, to bring to pass immortality and eternal life for you. You are, that you might have joy.

NOTES

1. Richard M. Weaver, *Ideas Have Consequences* (Chicago: University of Chicago Press, 1948; paperback edition 1984), 3-4.

2. Sam B. Gill, "Disenchantment," *Parabola* 1:13.

3. D. M. Dooling, "The Way Back," *Parabola* 10:49.

4. Ann Belford Ulanov, *Receiving Woman: Studies in the Psychology and Theology of the Feminine* (Philadelphia: Westminster Press, 1981), 174.

5. Ibid., 176.

6. Northrop Frye, *The Great Code: The Bible and Literature* (New York: Harcourt Brace Jovanovich, 1981), 231.

7. Rollo May, *Love and Will* (New York: W. W. Norton, 1969; paper ed., Dell Publishing, 1984), 307.

8. Joseph Fielding Smith, ed., *Teachings of the Prophet Joseph Smith* (Salt Lake City: Deseret Book, 1939), 241.

9. Brigham Young et al., *Journal of Discourses*, 26 vols. (Liverpool: F. D. and S. W. Richards, 1854-86), 9:3.

10. Frye, 168.

14.
Enlarging the Mormon Vision of Christian Ethics

L. Jackson Newell

MORMONS HAVE EARNED A REPUTATION FOR BEING INDUSTRIOUS, orderly, and honorable. For the most part this reputation is deserved. Despite our radical origins and global aspirations, we are also regarded as being provincial, conservative, and preoccupied with our own welfare. This reputation too is generally well deserved. In grappling with these different perspectives, I have concluded that geographical and cultural conditions have biased our moral consciousness toward immediate and personal concerns at the expense of long-range or global issues. But our doctrines may require more of us than we have thought.

Mormons more than most Christians attach great significance to specifics of personal behavior. As gatekeepers of the temples, bishops interview members regularly to ascertain their compliance with prescribed standards ranging from monetary contributions and diet to private vestments and personal habits. Those who don't pass muster are denied the privilege of temple attendance.[1] This procedure probably encourages self-discipline and sacrifice for the common good, but it can also produce a false sense of worthiness. The checklist approach may tempt us to be satisfied with the least we must do to meet the standard, and rob us of the ultimate challenge of Christian living—that of seeing the deepest needs of others on our own and acting upon our best instincts to help them. Fixed upon the letter, we can miss the spirit. When this happens our view becomes myopic and our actions, though sincere, may lack compassion.

Our social ethics, our sense of responsibility for other people in other places, often suffer some neglect due to our preoccupation with personal ethics. As a people we are relatively unconcerned about our natural environment, the arms race, human rights, and problems associated with world population growth, malnutrition or starvation. There are no doubt a number of factors that contribute to such insularity.

As religions go Mormonism is an all-encompassing style of life. The church touches and influences almost every aspect of our experience and commands much of our attention and energy. From what we drink and how we dress to where we spend our time and whose ideas we are likely to consider, our religion influences us to an unusual degree. I continue to be baffled by the extent to which Mormon intellectuals are engrossed in Mormon-related questions. Even those who are disaffected often remain obsessed with church issues more than with world or national concerns. Regardless of status or station, Mormons often feel the press of their culture to the point of saturation. The overwhelming majority of General Authorities still rise from Great Basin roots. Well-traveled as they are, they tend to see the world not only from an LDS perspective but also from a middle class, Western American vantage point. Geographical isolation is reinforced by a rather monolithic social structure. These two factors then, *saturation* and *isolation*, have given Mormonism a distinctive character. Fascinating as these cultural characteristics are, my primary purpose is to examine how they have influenced LDS theology.

Mormon leaders since Joseph Smith have taught that the Church of Jesus Christ of Latter-day Saints is a restoration of the doctrinal and institutional intent of the Savior himself. Members and leaders frequently testify to their belief that "the church is true" and that it is directed by heavenly revelation. Mormons also believed that the authority to act in God's name, the holy priesthood, came as part of the restoration in the time of Joseph Smith. These are powerful claims, and they have great importance for and influence upon those who accept them. But accepting them means different things to different people.

For many leaders and members, the concept of "the true church" means not only that the doctrine reflects the Lord's precise purposes and understandings but also that the judgments of church leaders are flawless and that the institution cannot err. Associated with this view is the notion that the LDS church is "right" and other churches are "wrong." The late apostle Bruce R. McConkie's unfortunate (and since retracted) reference to Catholicism as "the great and abominable church" typifies this dualistic interpretation of doctrine.[2] From this theological perspective, you either have truth or you don't.

A contrasting idea is that truth comes from many sources and that larger understandings arise gradually. Historical documents and prophetic writings contain references to the concept that truth is only partly known and that the church's quest to expand its doctrine is ongoing. For instance, Joseph Smith reported that part of the Book of Mormon was sealed due to his and his followers' unreadiness to comprehend or act upon its principles,[3] and the thirteenth Article of Faith emphasizes the existence of the good, the true, and the beautiful in the larger world — and our duty to embrace truth and goodness wherever they are found. Further, the doctrine of continuing revelation emphasizes the fluid and growing nature of LDS theology. For Latter-day Saints embracing these concepts, Mormonism may be viewed as "more true" and other bodies of religious doctrine as "less true." Hugh B. Brown, a counselor to church president David O. McKay, gave expression to this view when he addressed a convocation at Brigham Young University in 1969: "We have been blessed with much knowledge by revelation from God which, in some part, the world lacks. But there is an incomprehensibly great truth which we must yet discover. Our revealed truth should leave us stricken with the knowledge of how little we really know. It should never lead us to an emotional arrogance based upon a false assumption that we somehow have all the answers — that we in fact have a corner on the truth. For we do not."[4]

With these contrasting threads in our doctrine, Mormons vary considerably in their instinctive response to the unspoken question: "How true is the truth?" For some people truth is a complete and indivisible whole. Others feel that our knowledge is only partial, that the quest continues. Thus two Mormons equally committed to their religion may have quite different ideas about the nature of its claims. As a consequence they will likely hold sharply contrasting views about the world and their place in it. Some will be satisfied with the pronouncements of church leaders alone, convinced they have all the information necessary to act wisely, while others will seek understanding from many quarters.

A related question asks how God acts in human affairs. Agreeing on the existence of a personal God, one who loves and cares about us individually, we may still come to quite different conclusions about how he shows his concerns for us. The following questions pose three possibilities. (1) Does the Lord intervene in our ordinary affairs, blessing or chastening us daily for our thoughts and actions? (2) Does he focus his attention on great issues of mercy and justice and exert his influence indirectly through us? (3) Has he given us a world, some principles to follow, and a fair amount of intelligence—and the task of making the most of it? If we respond yes to the first question, the scope of our concern will be narrow. If we react more favorably to the second or third question, our horizons will expand as well as our sense of responsibility for our earth, for other peoples, and for future generations.

Neither scriptures nor contemporary LDS leaders provide a definitive answer about which interpretation of God's methods is more valid. Are we given basic principles and expected to govern ourselves, as Joseph Smith so explicitly encouraged us to do?[5] Or are we rewarded and punished regularly as a means of correcting our course? Is a good break in family finances a result of faithful tithe paying? Are adverse local weather conditions a reminder of our collective iniquities? If so then how does the faithful tithe payer explain an unfortunate or inexplicable business loss, or how do we interpret good rainfall and a bounteous harvest?

The important question is not whether deity can or does bless and discipline humanity, but how we view our relationship to deity. Do we expect and find gentle or not-so-gentle buffetings at every turn in the road to help us measure our course—and thus tune our consciousness to receive these promptings from our immediate experience? Or do we attune our consciousness to lasting ideas, Christian ideals, including the needs of unseen others within our gaze, and monitor our progress by enduring standards of mercy and justice? No one is blind to immediate concerns, and few are ignorant of global issues. Most of us are somewhere in the middle. But I do believe that our assumptions about God's role in our affairs can bend our vision either inwardly or outwardly.

At this point it may be appropriate to consider the relationship between the two theological issues considered above and the attitudes Mormons may have towards four overarching ethical problems in the larger society. I will consider in turn starvation and malnutrition, human rights, the arms race, and our relationship to the natural environment.

If one takes quite literally (and liberally) the injunction to multiply and replenish the earth and if one believes that the Lord is in control and will provide, then one is unlikely to become very concerned about overpopulation, malnutrition, or mass starvation. Such a person's faith suggests that the millennium will come or even that agricultural technology will reap unimaginable harvests from the sea. To this Latter-day Saint, family planning is simply evidence of flagging faith or misguided concern. On the other hand, if one believes we are responsible for this planet as trustees and deity is interested in our capacity to manage our resources, then population growth and malnutrition become important problems indeed. This second person will seek knowledge that may be helpful to understand the magnitude and potential of malnutrition and starvation and pray for the wisdom and strength to make a difference. In contrast the first person may be tempted to leave the fate of the victims of the expanding Sahara to the Lord. For a church that is expanding at a phenomenal pace in Latin America and aspires to do the same in Asia and Africa, what is believed and taught about birth control is much more than a personal matter.[6] Our doctrines and how we interpret them may have a direct bearing upon the health and welfare of literally billions around the globe.

Turning from biological rights to civil entitlements, it seems that many Mormons are inclined to await instructions from their church leaders before becoming politically involved. Reflecting the dominant middle-class values of contemporary Mormon culture and the embarrassment of earlier persecutions over polygamy, however, the LDS church has been reluctant to associate itself with controversial social movements. As a result the civil rights movement of the 1950s and 1960s, despite its quest for racial justice, went its full course with hardly a whimper of support from the LDS community — with a few notable exceptions. To a people who commit themselves to obeying, honoring, and sustaining secular law, civil disobedience may be somewhat repugnant. On the other hand, the denial of justice to a significant portion of the population on capricious grounds should be even more repugnant. When Latter-day Saints felt that justice was denied them in the last century, they chose to observe what they believed to be a higher law and willfully accepted prison sentences or asylum in other countries as the consequence. One could conclude that we will use civil disobedience in our own behalf but deny the use of this strategy when others seek justice. Certainly we are all more patient when someone else is suffering ills than when it is we ourselves. This natural human tendency was accentuated, however, in the case of the Mormons.

The 1978 revelation making the priesthood available to all worthy males may or may not have reflected the larger social milieu of the times, and it certainly *was* a giant step toward universal brotherhood in the LDS church, but it does not obscure the fact that Latter-day Saints generally ignored and still remain somewhat hostile to equal rights and opportunities for all men and women under the law. Unfortunately, some of our dominant theological interpretations may lead to perilous questions. Were the legal and social deprivations of the black community tolerated or even willed by the Lord because of previous or present unrighteousness? If I pay tithing, do missionary work, and otherwise meet the standard of a worthy Latter-day Saint, haven't I really dispatched my duty? Such are the moral dangers of taking too literally the doctrine of a caring God. We needn't care ourselves.

Similar patterns of belief may govern Mormon attitudes towards armaments control and environmental protection. We place trust in doctrinal assumptions that may be unwarranted, and we run risks as a result. Again dualistic thinking and a belief that God cares especially about us can lead to dangerous reasoning. If our nation is a chosen one and if its basic documents are inspired, as we Mormons are taught, then can any sum spent on defense be too great? If we do our part by building better and more accurate missiles and bombs, would an omnipresent father let an accident happen that would obliterate millions of Americans? Those who instinctively answer these questions in the affirmative will see no reason for SALT talks or other sincere efforts to reduce the perils of militarism.

Environmental protection is hardly an issue with those who see the Millennium around the corner. Nor is it likely that leaders or members of an expanding, economically pressed religious community will place the long-term benefits of a rich natural habitat above the advantages of cheaper fuel or the promise of higher tithing receipts. When practical problems confront people, they look for philosophical justifications to do what needs to be done — a process that is especially perilous when fundamental issues are at stake. It has always been so. Mormons can undoubtedly find in their theology concepts that help them justify exploitation of the environment, individually and collectively. But the environmental issue is an issue of time, short-term versus long-range. Those who take too literally the notion that "these are the last days" may nourish their present by robbing their posterity.

I have attempted to explore some of the reasons that Latter-day Saints are too often apathetic about facing some of the overarching moral and ethical problems of our time. My purpose has not been to denigrate the service Latter-day Saints render to the larger world nor to deny their considerable altruism. Through the LDS welfare system, we often contribute strategic service to those suffering disasters in other parts of the world, and many lives have been made richer and more meaningful through the missionary efforts of our people. I see no reason, however, why these good works should preclude a conscious and vital concern about the issues of liberty and justice around the globe that beg for understanding among a talented, well-traveled, and affluent people like the Mormons. In addition to trying to build the Mormon faith in South Africa, will we be part of the problem or part of the solution when it comes to respecting human rights in that country today? Here in America will the LDS church as an institution and will we as individuals do everything we can to assure that women's rights are secured fully and equally with or without the proposed constitutional amendment? Are we as individuals or is the church willing to forego economic advantages in order to protect the biosphere and the opportunities of future inhabitants of the earth?

There are hopeful signs. Once the June 1978 revelation was announced, Mormon leaders moved immediately to extend missionary work to black communities and to include black men and women in temple ordinances. Later a statement of the First Presidency about the MX missile spoke forcefully about the moral perils of the arms race in general. (Unfortunately much of the national press ignored this fact and interpreted the statement as self-serving regionalism.)

As Mormonism becomes a worldwide religion, individual members should re-examine the relationships between the historical and geographical factors that have shaped their cultural values and the unique theological claims that require a larger vision. Given the existence of contrasting interpretations of the restoration and of the way God manifests his concern for us, we should look afresh at our doctrine and ask if prevailing assumptions about it properly inform our efforts to "be our brother's keeper" in a global age. In the long run some of our assumptions will prove more correct than others. Therefore, we must each ask, "What are the consequences for me and for the world if the set of assumptions about theology that I have accepted prove to be less accurate than the alternatives?" If we ravage the earth, poison our lakes, and render the air unbreathable — and the Millennium doesn't come soon — what then?

As members of a rapidly expanding church living in a time when revolutions in technology are shrinking the earth, I believe it is essential that we reconsider our attitudes toward other societies and our commitments to temporal justice. Perhaps it is time we overcome the inertia of our historic isolation and fight the tendency (so accentuated by the comprehensiveness of our theology and culture) to become preoccupied with ourselves. More than either of these, however, we may need to re-examine our theological assumptions and renew our commitment to underlying Christian principles. Returning to the source of our faith may inspire new insights, and determination to open our windows to the larger world cannot help but enrich us. Modestly, we might even hope, we can be of some help.

NOTES

1. Since marriages are performed in the temple, denial of temple privileges can mean that parents are unable to attend the weddings of their children. Non-compliance with any of a number of specific standards can bar one from church leadership positions.

2. Bruce R. McConkie, *Mormon Doctrine* (Salt Lake City: Bookcraft), 1966). This reference does not appear in any subsequent editions.

3. *History of the Church*, Vol. 1.

4. *Church News*, 24 May 1969.

5. John Taylor quoted Joseph Smith as saying, "I teach them correct principles and they govern themselves" (*Latter-day Saints' Millennial Star* 13 [Nov. 1851]: 339).

6. See the *Ensign*, Aug. 1979, 23.

15.
"In Jeopardy Every Hour"

Susan B. Taber

A woman when she is in travail hath sorrow, because her hour is come (John 16:21).

WHEN MY TWO-AND-A-HALF-YEAR OLD DAUGHTER ABIGAIL AND I went to the hospital, I left the pie crusts and rolls I had mixed up that morning on the kitchen table along with the dress pattern I had bought for my new niece. It had been months since I had felt this energetic, and so that morning I had begun a few projects while I waited for our sixth child to be born. The telephone awakened me from my after-lunch nap; the pediatrician wanted to to discuss Abby's blood test results.

The day before he had said that the intermittent fever and leg pains which had plagued her for the previous four days might be symptoms of a bone infection, and he had ordered x-rays and a blood test. Since Abby now seemed much better, I hoped that he had found that she did not have a bone infection but something that could be treated with pink medicine at home. I held her on what was left of my lap, with my chin resting in her soft curls, as Dr. Miller explained that since her white count was 30,000, she probably had leukemia, and he wanted me to take her to the hospital that afternoon.

Although I was already halfway to the hospital in Wilmington, I returned to our home in Newark to grab some clothes and our toothbrushes. I punched down the still-rising dough and left a note on the front door directing the four older children to a neighbor's house. Before I picked up my husband Doug from the university, he left a note on the door of the seminar room cancelling the Institute class I was supposed to teach.

At the hospital I recited Abby's medical history over and over as she was examined by a nurse, a medical student, a resident, and two hematologists. Doug went home to take care of the other children. Several blood samples were drawn; we were sent downstairs for a chest x-ray; I held her hand while the IV was started. At nine o'clock Abby's nurse gave her an orange popsicle and pinned her armboard to the sheet so that the IV could not come loose. I eased my unwieldy body onto the cot which she'd pulled out of a chair for me and tried to comprehend what the hematologists had told me.

Ten years earlier I had sat silently weeping in St. Luke's Hospital, New York. Nine-month-old John, our first born, had been admitted for tests because of his enlarged spleen and liver. After the pediatrician had informed me that the bone marrow test was "suspicious," I sat wishing Eve had never bitten the apple and trying to prepare myself to give John back to God. My week of anguish before the doctors released John without a diagnosis had taught me a powerful lesson. Doug had administered to John the first night in the hospital and had blessed him that whatever had been wrong with him was gone and that he would be fine. I, however, had expended all my emotional energy trying to prepare for the worst and had found little comfort in the blessing. I would not make that mistake now. Since that time my faith in Doug's priesthood—based not only on the often prophetic character of the blessings he pronounced but also upon his daily prayer and scripture study—had increased. When Doug and I had administered to Abby the day before, he had said that her intermittent fever was caused by an infection and would go away when the infection subsided. She must, therefore, I reasoned, not have leukemia but something else. I resented every painful procedure and every beep of the IVAC that was making it impossible for me to sleep.

Doug had also given me a blessing that morning and had admonished me to develop my own spiritual resources. He had said that many would turn to me for wisdom and for strength. Neither, certainly, was in evidence now. I was out of control. Before morning I had to regain my composure or I would not be of any use to Abby.

Opening my Bible, I turned to the Sermon on the Mount. Suddenly the meaning of the "lilies of the field" came clear. I understood that Christ doesn't mean for us to go without clothing or to be slovenly, but rather that our persons as children of God are so glorious, so exquisitely wonderful that clothing and all our other acquisitions are truly superfluous. At last I was able to pray for strength to help Abby through the bone marrow aspiration and lumbar puncture scheduled for the morning.

We were busy the next day. The Mormon hotline must have hummed all night, for visitors came in all day long. Our home teacher arrived even before Dr. Benzel, a hematologist, came to perform the bone marrow. Doug said that casseroles were being brought in for him and the children. When he arrived, mid-morning, we were sent to see a woman whose name tag identified her as "Charlotte Sheehan: Pastoral Services: Parent Liaison." Doug brushed her off by saying that since the diagnosis wasn't confirmed, it was pointless to discuss how we were going to deal with leukemia at this time. I didn't want to talk to her either. There was no way she could understand the reality of the blessing which Abby had been given. To let her be helpful, Doug said he would appreciate some information to read if Abby did have leukemia. We agreed there was no point in calling either set of grandparents in Salt Lake City and Seattle yet. When we knew for sure this evening, we would tell the children and call our parents.

Dr. Benzel returned late in the day as I was trying to maneuver two dinner trays, a high chair, Abby, and all her tubes in the small open area of the room. As I squeezed catsup from a plastic tube over Abby's french fries, he told me that she did indeed have leukemia. He asked me to call Doug to arrange a time when we could both talk to him. Doug had gone back to Newark, twenty miles away, and had been on alert at the university, but he could not come now until after he had fed the children and settled them down. When I flatly told him over the telephone that the diagnosis was definite, his faint "Oh" was like a physical blow. Impossibility became reality.

After dinner with our four oldest children—John, Alan, Lisa, and Christina—Doug drove into Wilmington again. Our home teacher also returned to help Doug administer to Abby. The blessing was very short; Doug said afterwards that he felt she had already been blessed to recover and he couldn't add to that. Dr. Benzel took us into the nurses' break room where he carefully explained the treatment protocol and the mechanism of her disease. He was quite encouraging and said that he'd rather she had leukemia than some of the other diseases he treats. Doug, ever the scientist, got him involved in a technical discussion of physiology and pharmacology. While he went to the nurses' station to sign the release forms, I went back into Abby's room. The IV therapist was all ready to give the first dose of vincristine. She didn't think the present IV was flowing well enough to inject something as caustic as vincristine, so she began to insert a new one. Four nurses held Abby down while the therapist repeatedly stabbed into her arm searching for a vein.

Finally, at midnight, it was all over and Abby and I could go to sleep. She awoke several times to use the toilet. Each time I crawled back into my cot I had to use deep breathing to become comfortable. Eventually it occurred to me that perhaps this was more than muscle strain and awkwardness. I went out into the hall where I could time my contractions. It was two a.m. and they were ten minutes apart. An hour later I called Doug and asked him to come and take me to the maternity hospital. The night nurses kept offering to call an ambulance, but I heroically refused. Nurses glided silently through half-opened doors to halt the insistent beeping of the IVACs. The cloud of cigarette smoke near the elevator had finally dispersed. The melodramatic qualities of the scene did not escape me. Here was an episode full of drama and pathos—the promise of new life in the very shadow of mortality.

Doug arrived at 3:45 a.m. Julie Ridge, our closest church neighbor, came with him to stay with Abby. On the way Doug ran several red lights and made a couple of illegal turns even though I insisted that it wasn't necessary; he secretly enjoyed speeding along through the deserted streets. I was excited by both the drama of being up all night and the nonchalance I was able to exude as an experienced mother. This was, after all, my sixth delivery, and I expected it to be quick and unmedicated.

The baby should have appeared by 6:00, but it didn't. Labor slowed and stopped; after two nights without sleep, my body could not continue. Finally, after a nightmare of pitocin and Demoral, I awoke briefly to see a baby boy on the bed with me, the umbilicus wrapped around his neck. He turned pink and cried, and I went back to sleep for the rest of the day. That night I recorded the experiences of the past two days in my journal and then added, "This is a time when our beliefs and philosophy are severely tested, and I must discipline my feelings and thoughts to reflect my testimony and the guidance of the Spirit—perhaps so I can have the Spirit."

Julie said that Abby's nurses were amazed by our support system. Doug took the two boys to stay with a ward family who happened to live on our school bus route. The girls went to stay with another neighbor and colleague of Doug's. Julie would spend another day with Abby while Doug made arrangements to come and stay with her while I recuperated. The Relief Society president halted the flow of casseroles since no one was home and arranged for women to help me when I was released from the hospital. The ward held a day of fasting and prayer for Abby, and the Primary children made cards and sent small gifts to her. We had lived in Delaware for just a year; and as willing arms picked up our duties and loving hearts shared our burdens, I felt that Abby belonged to the ward almost as much as to us. Three years earlier when in the fourth month of my pregnancy I had nearly lost her, our church friends in Tennessee had cared for the other children, brought in meals, and even helped us move across town. When she was finally born, I felt that the ward had sustained her life. Once again we were in the Lord's hands.

The telephone was almost an appendage. I spent hours listening to and cheering up the other children as well as consulting with Doug about arrangements for the month that we expected Abby to be in the hospital. I wanted their lives to be as normal as possible; the less disruption, I felt, the less they would worry about Abby or miss me. Our families called us and so did friends and relatives from Tennessee, where we had formerly lived. Over and over I comforted callers as I explained Abby's good chances for a remission. The more I said, the more I wondered if I were deluding myself. Was I really the pillar of strength that people said I was, or was I just not facing reality? Julie reassured me by telling me that when she was with Abby she felt the presence of the Comforter; Doug reminded me of his impression that she would recover.

By the fifth evening my post-partum euphoria had worn off. I was tired and scared. I had spent too much time talking and not enough time sleeping. An officious nurse who had not been on duty since Robert was born came in to discuss my plans. She was skeptical and told me to go home to bed before going to stay with Abby and to leave Robert with someone else.

Tuesday morning Robert wanted to nurse every half hour, and I could hardly get dressed or eat my own breakfast. Robyn, my visiting teacher, came at 8:30 to take me home where three other ward sisters were waiting to help me clean the house. One went to the store to buy disposable diapers, baby wipes, and other necessities while I sorted the laundry and packed. I got out clean sheets for all the beds, but I couldn't change Abby's new rainbow sheets. They had been a graduation-from-the-crib present; and although it had been only a week since she had slept in her new bed, we had entered a world forever altered.

Neighbors dropped by to bring the mail they had collected or just to say hello. They, too, marvelled at the Relief Society cleaning crew. Had I been less desperate I would have been humiliated by the overpopulated refrigerator and the sticky kitchen floor, but I was grateful for the clean rooms and fresh sheets which were tangible manifestations of the prayers offered by ward members. Although I had once been a Relief Society president, I gained a new appreciation for the power of organized religion. By noon the house was clean! Julie Ridge stayed behind to hang up Doug's shirts from the dryer and took a load of laundry to her house. Robyn, my visiting teacher, drove me back to the hospital so that Doug could teach his afternoon class.

The baby had been very cooperative. He had slept peacefully while I whirled through the house, and then had given me time to unpack and write in my journal that afternoon, but he refused to go to sleep again after his eleven p.m. feeding. After several hours of alternately nursing him and walking through the corridors with him, I finally remembered the bottle of formula which the hospital had sent home with him. I groped around the top shelf of Abby's locker until I found it. Two hours later, at 6:30, the phlebotomist arrived to draw blood for Abby's daily CBC, and a new day began.

And we end up making an incredible tragedy out of it, instead of being able to look at life as a challenge, we look at it as a threat. Instead of at the end of life celebrating all the things that we have been able to share and to give and receive, we mourn the loss as we drown ourselves in self-pity. And all great moments we, in a way, turn into tragedies. . . . Unconditional love. It's the only thing that helps you not only not to be afraid of living, but of dying (Elisabeth Kubler-Ross, "To Live Until You Die," transcript, *Nova*, PBS).

Gradually Abby, Robert, and I began to establish a routine. Abby enjoyed having Robert with her in her bed while we kept him awake in the mornings. Usually, the nurse bathed Abby while I bathed Robert from a small basin on the rolling bed-table. Afternoons we all slept, at least for a short time.

One night I read the books which the parent liaison, Charlotte Sheehan, had given Doug. They had depressed him, especially the sections on preparing children for death. From the maternity hospital I had tried to bolster his courage by stressing her 90 percent chance of achieving a remission. Had she been in a car accident, I reasoned, 90 percent would sound very good. I didn't realize until I read these pamphlets that only 50 percent of children with leukemia are actually still in remission after five years. In the case of most accidents or other illnesses, the time before it is known whether the child will survive is relatively short. In the case of cancer, even when in remission, there is no certainty that the danger period has passed. There are only statistical probabilities. I mustered every reason I could think of why Abby's chances should be better than 50 percent, but I cried too.

Autumn had fully come as the days stretched toward two weeks. The streets were covered with dead leaves. Many afternoons Doug drove in so he could relieve me while I took a walk. I hoped to regain my vitality as well as lose my baby fat. A favorite route led through a park along the Brandywine River where the trees were gloriously colored, though the wind was often bitter. One afternoon as I walked back up the hill to the hospital, the street was suddenly flooded with light, and a strong feeling of peace and hope came over me. I felt that whatever happened, my test would not be losing Abigail. When I told Doug about it, he said that it was most important that we help Abby love life and develop a healthy personality in spite of the years of treatment ahead of her.

One afternoon I happened to watch a television program about the work of Elisabeth Kubler-Ross. I was deeply moved by her emphatic affirmation of the importance of life, even under the most difficult of circumstances, and of the possibilities for hope and fulfillment even while dying. My tears were not only of pity for her patients and their families and myself but also of gratitude for the eternal aspects of life which she espoused: love, service, honesty, and acceptance.

Abby had been hospitalized for just two weeks when her doctors decided that she was doing well enough to go home and finish her chemotherapy as an outpatient. They performed another bone marrow aspiration and lumbar puncture, but now I was allowed to stay in the room with her. At first I wondered if she would feel that I was an accessory to the pain that was inflicted upon her if I stayed with her, but she allowed me to comfort her during both procedures. I have since found that my being there has helped Abby endure these procedures and express her feelings freely. She learned to trust me as I learned to tell her exactly what would happen each day. After she learned what to expect, she did not cry or fuss until the actually painful part. More than once, the doctor, nurse, and I all ended up with tears of admiration in our eyes.

We all came home from the hospital after an absence of seventeen days on Doug's birthday. The after-school sitter had baked him a cake, and Doug's sister and family from Texas visited us for the weekend. My heart and eyes followed Abby as she silently moved from room to room Saturday morning, quietly playing in each of her favorite haunts. Now that I was sleeping in my own bed, my tense shoulders began to relax and my head stopped aching. The worst was behind us! We had come through relatively unscathed.

The next week we drove to the hospital three times for chemotherapy. Robert usually slept in his infant seat during the procedures. Then I'd wake him and nurse him during the hour that Abby was being observed for possible allergic reactions. Neighbors brought in dinners on our commuting days, and the children helped keep the house straight and fold diapers for Christmas spending money. On the last night of the induction phase of chemotherapy, Abby woke up crying with the pain in her legs. We had expected that the bone marrow aspiration scheduled for the next day would reveal that she was in remission. Why was she having bone pain now for the first time in four weeks? She must have relapsed already or not even have gone into remission. As I knelt beside her bed trying to comfort her, Abby seemed like a changeling. Her face and body were bloated from the prednisone, and there were bald streaks among her honey-colored curls. Of what use had all this treatment been? When I went back to my room, I pled with the Lord for her life, carefully adding, "Thy will be done."

In the morning Dr. Benzel was jubilant. "We did it!" He said just to give Abby some Tylenol for future bone pain. When I called my parents that night, my mother's relief was audible. Her sister Fern had died twenty-two years earlier of leukemia. My father sounded for the first time as if he thought Abby had any hope of being cured.

We had celebrated our son Alan's birthday in Abby's hospital room and Lisa's a week after we came home. Thanksgiving was another strictly family day. Because of Abby's suppressed immune system, we had neither invited nor been invited as guests. I spent the day preparing a traditional turkey dinner complete with two kinds of pie and broccoli, which was miraculously still growing in the garden. As I worked, I felt gratitude for Abby's life, especially toward all the parents who had allowed their children to receive experimental treatment. Without the things that had been learned from their suffering, we would not have any hope of keeping Abby with us. I thought about Keats a lot, too. A tinge of mortality certainly did add a poignant zest to life.

Except for vincristine which she received once every four weeks at the doctor's office, Abby's medications were all given by mouth. Every Tuesday I took her to a nearby laboratory for a blood test; then the nurse would telephone that afternoon to give me the dosage levels for the coming week. She also had a weekly lumbar puncture with methotrexate to prevent meningeal leukemia.

Dr. Bean, the neurologist, always seemed very concerned about the effects of Abby's illness on the rest of the family. I always assured him, somewhat defensively, that we were all communicating with each other just fine. "Sometimes," he told me, "fathers escape by going to work. It's an acceptable way to be less involved." I felt satisfied with Doug's level of participation but found myself increasingly short-tempered on Wednesday mornings. By the seventh time I didn't want to go alone, so I insisted that Doug come with us.

By the time Dr. Bean arrived, Doug was quite impatient, Robert had slept too long, and Abby and I had exhausted all our amusements. I was helping the nurse hold Abby in position when Dr. Bean asked, "Are you all right?" I looked up, startled, but he wasn't talking to me. Doug was very pale and began talking in the fast, incoherent way he does when I'm in labor. Dr. Bean asked him to lie down, but Doug said he'd just walk around until he felt better. Finally he did sit down. Afterwards Doug claimed he hadn't been upset. Dr. Bean asserted that he had been affected more than he'd realized. Later at home Doug and I shared our sorrow; I realized that we had been so busy coping that we really hadn't had time to share our feelings.

> And his disciples asked him, saying, Master, who did sin, this man, or his parents, that he was born blind? (John 9:2)

Robert's one-month weight gain was less than it should have been, though Dr. Cohn commended me for keeping up the breast-feeding in spite of our hectic medical schedule. "I guess you could even nurse in a telephone booth," he remarked. He also said that it was hard to understand why illnesses such as leukemia had to strike such nice families. "Perhaps," he ventured, "it is because they have the strength to handle it better than others."

When the incomprehensible happens, we seem compelled to explain it. When my uncle drowned during polio therapy, my parents explained that he must have fulfilled his earthly mission and had gone on a heavenly one. My eight-year-old mind could not quite understand how Heavenly Father could need Uncle Bill in the spirit world more than my aunt and six cousins needed him; but when I was fourteen, I accepted Aunt Fern's death as a release from her sufferings, wondering only why a God who had created the world had also created such suffering.

When I read Sterling McMurrin's *Theological Foundations of the Mormon Religion* for an Institute class my junior year in college, I eagerly embraced the concept of a nonabsolute God who had created neither evil nor suffering but was in fact involved in overcoming both. My anguish over John had largely been a struggle to accept emotionally this philosophy. Although I had realized that I would have been at peace if my faith had been stronger, I had been grateful for the spiritual watershed of that experience.

> All these things shall give thee experience and shall be
> for thy good (D&C 122:7).

Someone in our ward philosophized that this had happened to make us a better family. How can I accept a divine program of family improvement predicated on the suffering of a two-year-old? I could find no reason other than the laws of probability for Abby's illness. Even the first night in the hospital I had been acutely aware of how fortunate Doug and I had been during our lives. Since then in almost every situation, I could see the Lord blessing and helping us. It reminded me of the week a few years before when all four children and I had been ill while I was working on a major church assignment. I had been very aware of receiving just enough strength to get through each day and had felt the spirit guide me as I decided how to spend my limited energy.

Our goal now was life as usual, though there were adjustments. Since Abby could not go into stores, I had a sitter come in twice a week so I could run errands. I had resumed teaching Institute even before we came home, but on Sundays Doug and I split up for church. I took the older children and went to choir practice and sacrament meeting. Doug and I switched places during Sunday School and then he taught the deacons' quorum and brought everyone home.

Doug and I had always been active, almost to the point of fanaticism, but I found it surprisingly easy to sink into my bed after feeding Abby and Robert while the rest of the family was still at church. Singing in the choir became one of the pillars of my spiritual life. Most of my journal writing was done in doctors' waiting rooms. One day I recorded in a confused metaphor that I felt as if I were spinning dizzily on a speeding downhill roller coaster. One day feeling unable to concentrate on any of the tasks at hand, I went into the bedroom to pray. As I knelt to beg for help, I felt that instead I should express gratitude for my blessings. Suddenly in the middle of giving thanks for Doug and for my children, I caught a glimpse of the eternal glory of their spirits. On Christmas day, we were all able to attend church for the first time in two months.

> If in this life only we have faith in Christ, we are of all
> men most miserable. But now is Christ risen from the dead,

and become the first fruits of them that slept (1 Cor. 15:19-20).

The next Sunday though I had to take Abby to the doctor while the others went to church. Her high fever was not responding to the antibiotic prescribed the day before. When the pediatrician saw the infected-looking blisters on her fingers and legs he thought she had chicken-pox, often deadly to children on chemotherapy. As I drove home to pack, I prayed, "Why does Abby have to suffer so much? What purpose is there to all this?" The thought formed whole in my mind, "The bonds between you and Abby will be stronger even than death." Before Doug took us to the hospital, he and Doug Ridge administered to her as she sat in her high chair. Doug "rebuked" the infection and said she would soon be well.

We were ushered into a tiny isolation cubicle with two cribs but with no telephone, television, or privacy. The outside window overlooked the cemetery. The doctors prescribed antibiotics and acyclovir through the IV while they tried to find out what she had. Drugs were injected into the solution practically every hour of the day and night. By Tuesday the infection was flourishing, and I wondered when it would be "rebuked." A huge pustule had appeared on her leg, making ten or twelve large ones all together. I wept in the shower; I sobbed aloud walking beside the frozen Brandywine River. Wednesday night when a rash broke out on Abby's legs and feet, I was afraid she had toxic shock. The cultures eventually grew staph, and the doctors began to believe that she did not have chicken pox. One of them told me that on a healthy person her raging infection would have been a mere pimple.

As I watched over her Thursday morning, grateful that her temperature was no longer climbing between 104 and 105, I envisioned her peacefully asleep in a coffin. When I raised the window blind, there were grave diggers actually digging across the street. Expecting poor Yorick's skull to be tossed up at any moment, I leaned my head into the corner and quietly let self-pity and despair wash over me. It had been easy to be brave during the two months when things were going according to plan, but I had wondered if I could be so if they weren't. I was embarrassed when the head nurse came in and sent me to talk with Charlotte Sheehan; I had been found out, but I was not willing to reveal what I felt was my abysmal lack of faith. After Charlotte told me that she had lost a child to Tay-Sachs disease, I was able to share with her my concerns about John's anger and Lisa's frequent headaches. Eventually I explained that I did believe that Abby would recover, but that I was having a hard time keeping that faith strong.

That evening we were moved to a larger room on the regular floor. Abby rode regally in a small wheel-chair; and as soon as we were settled, she demanded and ate two bowls full of the Cheerios which Doug had brought from home. It was another full week, though, before she was strong enough to go home. We had spent exactly a month out of the preceding two and a half months residing in hospitals. Robert now slept through the night, and Abby expected to have all my time and attention. Now I knew why the doctors had told us to call at the first sign of any illness. In February Abby developed pneumonia and I felt that my promptness in calling the doctor for an antibiotic had made it possible for her to be treated at home instead of in the hospital.

I kept busy to avoid brooding, but I was always aware that I might not be able to fulfill my commitments. All my life I had projected myself into the future; now the present was everything— the future nothing. Easter Sunday took me by surprise. Practicing the music had soothed and elated me, but that morning I discovered a new dimension of the gospel. I had struggled for years to understand the Atonement, but that day the promise of the resurrection resonated through my soul, and I realized that I apprehended it in a way that had not been accessible to me before.

And why stand we in jeopardy every hour? (1 Cor. 15: 30)

At the beginning of May, Dr. Benzel increased Abby's chemotherapy to the level that had wiped out her white count at New Year's. I was apprehensive all month, but nothing happened until the second Saturday in June. After a picnic and a swim, Abby seemed very tired. By morning her temperature was 103, and since her white count was very low, she had to go to the hospital. This time, however, after we had moved in, they told the doctor that Robert couldn't stay with us. How could even the Relief Society take care of a seven-month-old baby who would not take a bottle, and how would I survive? Eventually they relented, but I knew I would have to start weaning Robert.

I was chagrined to find my faith plummeting as Abby's temperature rose and stayed above 104. Although she really was not as ill as in January, her temperature stayed high for several days. Was she in greater danger than I had supposed? I prayed constantly that her fever would break. The words of the blessing that Doug had given her came into my mind as I pled with the Lord. He had promised her that she would be able to rest, eat, and drink as she needed to get well. She was doing none of those. That afternoon, I decided, I would make sure she slept, at least. I rubbed her back and held her hand until she fell asleep. Several nurses came in and out, sometimes talking loudly and always leaving the door open when they left. I made a sign, "SLEEPING: Please keep door closed," and clipped it to the door. When Robert awakened from his nap, I took him into the hall for another hour while Abby slept. The nurse ordered popsicles and chocolate milk which I gave Abby at every opportunity. That afternoon her temperature did not go quite as high, and she was able to go to sleep more easily that night.

When her temperature had been normal for two days, I asked the hematologist if these infections were an expected part of therapy or if Abby were unusually susceptible. He looked down at the floor and then explained that their strategy is to keep her right on the edge. Infections come when the chemotherapy has been pushed too hard. "But," he added, "these are inevitable because if we didn't push too hard occasionally, she would not be getting enough chemotherapy."

Today the nurse removed the IV and tomorrow we'll go home. Again we pick up the threads of our life. Abby will tumble in the living room with her sisters, swing in the backyard, and in a few weeks go to the pool. I'd like to keep her in her own room like Rapunzel, but of course, I can't. Doug says he's realized that we have to think in terms of "when Abby is hospitalized again" not "if." My spirit continues its tightrope walk between hope and dread. While here I've read some of the Book of Mormon and reread my journal. It reminds me of the hope and comfort that surrounded us when Abby first became ill. I pray constantly that I correctly understand that spirit.

* * * * *

Just two years later, on 3 June 1986, Abby came home from the hospital for the last time. Leukemia had invaded her bone marrow in January and it had taken until the end of April to achieve another remission. She was immediately scheduled for a bone-marrow transplant in mid-June, the earliest possible time. On 8 May, however, Doug stated in a priesthood blessing that Abby would be happy "when she returned home to her Heavenly Father and would be glad to be there." He told me that he felt she had months, not years, left with us. I was anguished and when her bone marrow was completely clear two weeks later, mystified by the incongruity. The next week she was given another course of high dose ARA-C to maintain the remission, but just a week later there was leukemic cell in her daily CBC report. A bone marrow aspiration revealed that she had gone out of remission again. Since her doctors advised us that further treatment would not achieve a long-term remission, we brought her home to enjoy the summer with her family, friends, toys, and swing set.

On 7 August 1986, Doug and Doug Ridge administered to her for the last time. Half an hour later she died peacefully in her sleep.

Epilogue: "The Power of Faith"

Hugh B. Brown

... THE PREDOMINATE SENSE IN WHICH THE WORD *FAITH* IS USED throughout the scriptures is that of full confidence and trust in the being, purposes, and words of God. Such trust, if implicit, will remove all doubt concerning the things accomplished or promised of God, even though such things be not apparent or explicable by the ordinary senses. . . .

We do not teach the principle of faith merely for what it will do for one in the next world. We believe that there is real practical value in mental concepts which increase one's self respect and effectiveness here and now. . . .

Eternal life means more than merely continuing to exist. Its qualitative value will be determined by what we believe and do while in mortality and by our conformity to eternal law in the life to come. Eternal existence would be most undesirable if that existence became fixed and static upon arrival there. "It is hope and expectation and desire and something ever more about to be" that gives lilt and verve to mortal and immortal life. We cannot imagine, nor would we desire, an eternity without opportunity for growth and development. We believe in eternal progression.

Faith in God and the ultimate triumph of right contributes to mental and spiritual poise in the face of difficulties. It is a sustaining power when a confining or antagonistic environment challenges one's courage. Similarly if one has a vivid sense of his own divinity, he will not be easily persuaded to deprave his mind, debauch his body, or sell his freedom for temporary gain. Goethe is right when

171

he makes Mephistopheles, his devil, say, "I am the spirit of negation."
Negation always bedevils life.

Thus we recommend faith as a present, living power for
good here and now as well as for what it will do for us in achieving
salvation hereafter.

Wherever in life great spiritual values await man's appropri-
ation, only faith can appropriate them. Man cannot live without faith
because in life's adventure the central problem is character building—which is not a product of logic but of faith in ideals and sacri-
ficial devotion to them. The writer of the Epistle to the Hebrews saw
the intimate relationship between the quality of faith and the quality
of life and called upon his readers to judge the Christian life by its
consequences in character.

We cannot avoid looking ahead and to some degree basing
our activities upon things which we cannot see. But bit by bit we gain
assurance. We have some knowledge of what that is and of what has
been. But it is necessary that we have faith in that which is yet to come.

In this universal venture of life, its full meaning can be
understood only by the application of faith, wherein the best treasures of the spirit are obtainable only through courageous open-
heartedness and the kind of character which is possible to all men of
deep conviction.

But every discussion of faith must distinguish it from its
caricatures. Faith is not credulity. It is not believing things you know
are not so. It is not a formula to get the universe to do your bidding.
It is not a set of beliefs to be swallowed up by one gulp. Faith is not
knowledge; it is mixed with lack of understanding or it would not be
faith. Faith does not dwindle as wisdom grows.

Above all faith is to be contested with pessimism and cyni-
cism. Those who say they have become disillusioned with life are lost
without faith. Faith is confidence in the worthwhileness of life. It is
assurance and trust. Perhaps the greatest contrast to faith is fear.
Jesus often said to his followers: "Be not afraid. . . . "

To believe that we do not stand alone, that we are fellow
laborers with God, our *human* purposes comprehended in *his* purposes—God behind us, within us, ahead of us—this is the solid rock
upon which all rational religion rests. . . .

No message short of religion has ever met man's need in this
estate. Faith that God himself is pledged to the victory of righteous-

ness in men in the world, that he cares, forgives, enters into man's struggle with transforming power and crowns the long endeavor with triumphant character — such faith alone has been great enough to meet the needs of men.

When faith in God goes, man loses his securest refuge and must suffer. Strong men broken in health, men who have lost the fortunes of a lifetime, families with long illness, mothers who have wept at children's graves — these and other staggering blows test the faith of good and bad alike. Nothing but religious faith has been able to save men from despair. As Jesus said the rains descend and the floods come and the winds blow, whether man's house be built on rock or sand. It is faith which makes the difference. . . .

God help us to rise to a point where we can retain faith in the future, whatever it may hold. When suffering, we need most of all to remember there is an explanation, although we may not know exactly what it is.

Religious faith gives confidence that human tragedy is not a meaningless sport of physical forces. Life is not what Voltaire called it, "a bad joke"; it is really a school of discipline whose author and teacher is God.

Faith is a rod to truth, without which some truths can never be reached at all. The reason for its inevitableness in life is not our lack of knowledge but rather that faith is as indispensible as logical demonstration in any real knowing in the world. Faith is not a substitute for truth but a pathway to truth.

However undecided men may appear, they cannot altogether avoid decision on the main matter of religion. Life will not let them. For a while the mind may hold itself suspended between alternatives. The adventure of life goes on and men inevitably tend to live either as though the Christian God is real or as though he is not. This then is the summary of the matter. Life is a great adventure in which faith in God presents the issues of transcendent import. And on these issues life itself continually compels decisions. . . .

CONTRIBUTORS

Lavina Fielding Anderson, former associate editor of *Dialogue: A Journal of Mormon Thought,* is president of Editing, Inc. "The Ambiguous Gift of Obedience" was originally presented as part of a *Dialogue*-sponsored panel at the Sunstone Symposium, 24 August 1985, Salt Lake City, Utah, and subsequently published in *Dialogue: A Journal of Mormon Thought* 20 (Spring 1987): 136–44.

Arthur R. Bassett is Professor of Humanities at Brigham Young University. "How Much Tolerance Can We Tolerate?" was first published in *Sunstone* 11 (Sept. 1987): 22–29.

Irene M. Bates, a convert to Mormonism who joined the church in England in 1955, is currently a Ph.D. candidate in U.S. history at UCLA. "Another Kind of Faith" was first published in *Sunstone* 13 (Feb. 1989): 21–23.

Elouise M. Bell is a professor of English and Associate Dean of General and Honors Education at Brigham Young University. "The Better for My Foes: The Role of Opposition" first appeared in *Sunstone* 6 (Jan.–Feb. 1981): 18–22.

Hugh B. Brown, a General Authority of the Church of Jesus Christ of Latter-day Saints from 1958 until his death in 1975, served in the First Presidency from 1961–70. "The Power of Faith" was first delivered during the church's October 1969 General Conference and subsequently published in *Conference Reports*.

D. Jeff Burton, an engineering consultant living in Salt Lake City, is author of *For Those Who Wonder,* which is available at most LDS bookstores. "The Phenomenon of the Closet Doubter" was first published in *Sunstone* 7 (Sept.–Oct. 1982): 34–38.

Richard J. Cummings is Professor of French at the University of Utah. "Some Reflections on the Mormon Identity Crisis" was given as a presidential address at the Association of Mormon Letters in October 1979 and published in *Sunstone* 4 (Dec. 1979): 27–32.

Edwin B. Firmage is a professor of law at the University of Utah, co-author of *Zion in the Courts: A Legal History of the Church of Jesus Christ of Latter-day Saints,* and editor of *An Abundant Life: The Memoirs of Hugh B. Brown.* "Restoring the Church: Zion in the Nineteen and Twenty-first Centuries" was first published in *Sunstone* 13 (Feb. 1989): 33–40.

Scott G. Kenney, founding publisher of *Sunstone* magazine and Signature Books, edited the autobiography of E. E. Ericksen. "At Home at Sea: Confessions of a Cultural Mormon" first appeared in *Sunstone* 13 (June 1989): 16–20.

Betina Lindsey is a novelist, ward librarian, and graduate of Brigham Young University in English. "Woman as Healer in the Modern Church" was first presented at the Sunstone Symposium and then published in *Dialogue: A Journal of Mormon Thought* 23 (Fall 1990): 63–76.

Ron Molen, a retired architect, is author of *House Plus Environment.* "The Two Churches of Mormonism," presented at the Sunstone Symposium in 1988, is published here for the first time.

L. Jackson Newell is Professor of Higher Education at the University of Utah, and occasional essayist on philosophical and religious issues. "Enlarging the Mormon Vision of Christian Ethics" first appeared in *Sunstone* 7 (March–April 1982): 29–32.

Levi S. Peterson, a professor of English at Weber State University, is author of *Canyons of Grace, The Backslider,* and *Juanita Brooks: Mormon Woman Historian.* "A Christian by Yearning" was first published in *Sunstone* 12 (Sept. 1988): 19–22.

Linda Sillitoe is a journalist, writer, and editor. She is author of *Sideways to the Sun* and *Windows on the Sea and Other Stories,* and co-author of *Salamander: The Story of the Mormon Forgery Murders.* "The Ghost of the Pioneer Woman" is published here for the first time.

Susan B. Taber is finishing a doctorate in Mathematics Education at the University of Delaware. "In Jeopardy Every Hour" was first published in *Dialogue: A Journal of Mormon Thought* 19 (Winter 1986): 109–20.

Donlu D. Thayer, a housewife and mother of six children, is an editor and teacher at Brigham Young University. "Respite for a Heretic: Jesus Christ and the Language of Desire" was first published in *Sunstone* 12 (July 1988): 14–23.